SAY YES TO GOD

Mary and the Revealing of the Word Made Flesh

Edited by Martin Warner

Foreword by P. D. James

Tufton Books

Tufton Books
Faith House
7 Tufton Street
London SW1P 3QN

Tufton Books is an imprint of Church Union Publications

First published 1999

British Library Cataloguing in Publication Data

A catalogue record for this book is available from the British Library

ISBN 0-85191-229-X

Typeset by Phoenix Photosetting, Chatham, Kent
Printed and bound in Great Britain by
Redwood Books, Trowbridge, Wiltshire

Contents

List of Contributors   v

Foreword   vii

1. **Introduction** – Martin Warner   1

2. **Revealed in Doctrine**
   Rowan Williams   15
   *'The Seal of Orthodoxy': Mary and the Heart of
      Christian Doctrine*

3. **Revealed in Society**
   Elaine Appelbee   33
   Contemporary Issues for a Holy Family
   Stephen Cottrell   46
   Mary the Evangelist
   Madeleine Bunting   59
   Sacred Spaces in Secular Culture

4. **Revealed in Art**
   David Brown   69
   Mary's Discipleship and the Artistic Imagination
   Catherine Oakes   83
   *Reflections on the Iconography of the Virgin as a Figure
      of Divine Mercy in Medieval Art*
   Sarah Jane Boss   95
   Guardians of the Way

5. **Revealed in Liturgy**
   Michael Reardon   123
   *Icon of the Heavenly City: Towards an Understanding
      of the Gothic Cathedral*
   Ian Boxall   142
   Who is the Woman Clothed with the Sun?
   Timothy Jones   159
   The Built Heritage of the English Church

Colin Baldy   171
*Music and Devotion to Our Lady in the
   Anglican Tradition*
Stephen Platten   181
Cathedrals: Sacred Spaces and Common Ground

List of Contributors

Elaine Appelbee is a member of General Synod, Vice-Chair of its Board for Social Responsibility and a Church Urban Fund Trustee.

Colin Baldy is an opera singer, teacher and church musician. Since 1996 he has helped organize the music for the National Pilgrimage to Walsingham.

Sarah Jane Boss is Director of the Marian Study Centre, based at Ushaw College, Durham.

Ian Boxall teaches New Testament Studies at St Stephen's House and in the University of Oxford.

David Brown is Van Mildert Professor of Divinity in the University of Durham, and Residentiary Canon of Durham Cathedral.

Madeleine Bunting is Religious Affairs Correspondent of *The Guardian*.

Stephen Cottrell is a Missioner with Springboard, the initiative of the Archbishops of Canterbury and York for Evangelism.

Timothy Jones is Historic Buildings and Areas Inspector for English Heritage, with particular responsibility for listed buildings and conservation areas in the City of Westminster.

Catherine Oakes is the staff tutor for the Visual Arts in the Department for Continuing Education at the University of Bristol.

Stephen Platten is Dean of Norwich.

Michael Reardon is an architect in Warwickshire, specializing in the conservation and repair of historic buildings, and the design of spaces for the performing arts. He is Surveyor of the Fabric to both Hereford and Birmingham cathedrals.

Martin Warner is Priest Administrator of the Shrine of Our Lady of Walsingham.

Rowan Williams is Bishop of Monmouth in the Church in Wales, and a former Lady Margaret Professor of Divinity at the University of Oxford.

Foreword

P D James

No other woman in history has been more influential than Mary, the mother of Jesus Christ. Yet historically we know little about her, not her family, nor the date and place of her birth. To millions of Christians she is the immaculately conceived and virgin Mother of God, interceding to her Son on behalf of the living and the dying. For millions of others, of all faiths and none, she is the unknown and unknowable Jewish woman who gave birth to the teacher and healer whose short life and sacrificial death initiated one of the great religions of the world. She has inspired some of the world's greatest poetry, its most magnificent literature and most beautiful art. Throughout the generations, a picture of St Mary holding the Christ Child has been an icon of the pains and sacrifice of motherhood, as well as of its privileges and its joys.

To some modern feminists she is seen as an over-idealised representation of womanhood: submissive, unquestioning and ineffably pure; to million of others, both men and women, she remains the most powerful, the most comforting and the most human of the saints, embodying for all generations the virtues of love, self-sacrifice and perfect obedience to the will of God. It is small wonder that she has fascinated the human imagination for nearly two thousand years. No day passes throughout the world in which candles are not lit at her shrines, her name invoked and her intercession sought.

Pilgrimages have for generations been made to the legendary places associated with Mary. In England the most ancient, the most revered and the most frequently visited Marian holy place is Walsingham in Norfolk. Here kings, great Counsellors of State, priests, nuns and ordinary people have come since the 11th century in search of grace, comfort, healing and renewal of faith. The shrine was suppressed during the Reformation and the image of Our Lady burnt, but Walsingham itself could not be destroyed. It waited in patience and silence for its regeneration. This took 400 years, but it came.

I first went to Walsingham in Norfolk as a member of a coach party from a London church in the 1960s, but have made the journey several times since, usually with a friend as I don't drive. It is not an easy place to get to. There are no quick non-stop trains from London. But perhaps this inaccessibility is right; pilgrimage isn't a day's outing. A little trouble, a little time, a little seeking out are appropriate. Pilgrimages are all a joyous but important journey of discovery.

And on arrival one does indeed feel on holy ground. Here Anglicans and Roman Catholics, although they have different shrines, share a common devotion to the handmaid of the Lord. But it is not only lovers of Walsingham who will enjoy and be edified by this collection of essays, *Say Yes to God*; all who read these essays will be left with a deeper understanding, not only of the place of Mary in Christian theology, in art and in society, but of the mystery of the incarnation.

PART I

Introduction

Introduction

Martin Warner

'Mary said, "Behold, I am the handmaid of the Lord; let it be to me according to your word."' (Luke 1.38)

> At least we know for certain that we are three old sinners,
> That this journey is much too long, that we want our dinners,
> And miss our wives, or books, our dogs,
> But have only the vaguest idea why we are what we are.
> To discover how to be human now
> Is the reason we follow this star.
>
> (W. H. Auden, *For the Time Being*)

Whether you approach from the north, the south, or the west of England the story is the same. The roads get narrower and narrower, until even the lines down the middle disappear and ducks waddle contentedly in and out of the traffic, taking their place with coaches, cars, tractors and caravans. This is Walsingham; it's different. Perhaps it's unique.

The essays which follow were originally given as papers at a series of regional Day Conferences organized by the Shrine of Our Lady of Walsingham in Norfolk. Known as 'England's Nazareth', this small village has been a place of pilgrimage since the 11th century.

Historical Origins

The origins of pilgrimage devotion stem from the story that in 1061, Richeldis de Faverches, the Lady of the Manor of Walsingham, had a vision in which she was taken to Nazareth and shown the house of the Annunciation. She was instructed by the Blessed Virgin Mary to note the exact dimensions of the house and to build a replica.

Her son, Geoffrey de Faverches, entrusted the wooden house

built by Richeldis to his chaplain, Edwy, when he embarked on pilgrimage to the Holy Land. The Manor of Walsingham subsequently passed into the hands of the Clare family, who endowed the Shrine. At some stage in the early part of the second half of the 12th century, it passed into the care of Augustinian Canons.

Records indicate that Walsingham enjoyed a degree of royal favour. Henry III, Edwards I, II and III, Henry VI, Edward IV, Henry VII and, in his younger days, Henry VIII all came on pilgrimage. But the Reformation brought about the suppression of the Shrine. In 1538 the Augustinian Priory was surrendered. The image of Our Lady of Walsingham was taken to London and burnt at Chelsea. Pilgrimage ceased for nearly 400 years.

The 20th-century restoration of pilgrimage to both Anglican and Roman Catholic centres of devotion now brings many thousands to Walsingham each year. The Roman Catholic National Shrine is centred on the 14th-century Slipper Chapel of St Catherine, next to which is a beautiful and contemporary basilica, the Chapel of Reconciliation.

Anglican pilgrimage focuses on a restored Holy House in which sits a replica of the original image of Our Lady of Walsingham, copied from the seal of the pre-Reformation Priory. Both centres of devotion have their own story of restoration to tell, but perhaps more importantly, both draw pilgrims to an experience of the mystery of the Incarnation as it touches our lives today.

Say Yes to God

The scriptural examples of pilgrimage are invariably of a journey in which God reveals himself, often quite unexpectedly. Revelations on the Mount of Moriah, at Bethel, Peniel or Horeb have that same quality which the disciples experienced on the road to Emmaus. Revelation is the harvest of pilgrimage; pilgrimage, the nurture and preparation of revelation.

In 1928 the restorer of the Anglican Shrine, Fr Hope Patten, wrote in his introduction to the Pilgrim's Manual:

In these days of materialism, unbelief and indifference to Christianity, the value of such a Shrine cannot be over-estimated. Walsingham boldly witnesses to the truth of the Incarnation, to the indispensable part our Lord's Mother plays in God's plan for our salvation, to the reality of the life beyond the grave.

Pilgrimage is increasingly a way in which people seek to apprehend the mystery and reality of which Fr Patten wrote. 'To discover how to be human now is the reason we follow the star', in the words of W. H. Auden.

The particular revelation to which Walsingham bears witness is the annunciation; Gabriel's *Ave* and Mary's *fiat mihi*, her 'Yes to God'. Reflection on this event leads us to see it not so much as a chance encounter, but as a stage in those processes by which God draws us each to himself in his plan of salvation. Mary's 'Yes to God' is a statement about disposition and openness, one spiritual and decisive moment of revelation and response at a stage somewhere along her pilgrimage of faith.

The essays which follow offer further reflection on that process of revelation and response. The title, *Say Yes to God* points not only to Mary's experience, but also to our own progress along the pilgrimage of faith, to our aptitude for reception of God's self-disclosure, and the many different levels, ways and contexts in which we recognize and receive it.

Revelation in Doctrine

In this first section Rowan William's essay 'Mary, Seal of Orthodoxy' stands magnificently as a statement about the scope of our endeavour. It has within it that infusion of Trinitarian vision which both secures faith and confounds rationalism. The invitation he offers is to orthodoxy, which evokes the life of God and issues in holiness.

This may sound very laudable and attractive but, you might think, likely to be of more interest to the expert, i.e. someone else. Do not be misled. Doctrine is not for the experts; it is the way experts handle what Christians believe.

The revelation in this chapter is certainly to be found at the level of lucidity of thought, simply stated. But there is revelation in the texture of the thought itself. Here doctrine and devotion form the warp and weft of that faith which inspired the icon of the Mary, the Hodegetria, or the hymns of Charles Wesley and John Keble. Here the witness of the scriptures is coupled with chanting the *Salve Regina* before a statue of Our Lady, Seat of Wisdom.

Worship and spirituality feed off theological language and vice versa. Marian devotion has suffered in recent years from many of the reforms that have taken place in catholic practice and theological perception. The result is the danger that Mary becomes an extra, for those who like that sort of thing; a bit dated and of limited, if definite, appeal. No child views his or her mother in those terms.

Mary's place in the life of the Church, in the life of the Christian, flows from her place in Christian doctrine. Rowan Williams uses the term 'lifeblood' very aptly to describe this centrality. What we believe about Mary and our devotion to her should not therefore be an added doctrinal construct, like a special niche into which to fit a statue. Perhaps we should see her more as the very walls of our church building, within which the people of God find their true identity as Christ is brought to birth in their midst in word and sacrament – Mary, Mother of the Church and seal of orthodoxy.

Revelation in Society

Walsingham is a difficult place to get to. There is little or no public transport and the state of the roads has already been mentioned! Pilgrimage is therefore a social thing. It commits you to engagement with others, even at the remote and impersonal level of a queue of traffic behind a tractor.

For those who travel by coach or minibus the formation of a distinctive group, within which the needs of others have to be considered, offers at a human level a statement about the nature of community. If one person is lost, injured or delayed, all are affected. Like salvation, pilgrimage is not a private matter, although it may be intensely personal and very intimate.

Many pilgrim groups arrive in Walsingham on a Friday night and stay for the weekend. The journey is often a tiring one, but the transformation on their arrival is remarkable. Again, this is not necessarily the result of self-conscious spiritual exercise, but a human response at the physical and spiritual level to the beauty of God revealed in the very beautiful part of his creation which is North Norfolk.

This, surely, is also a sign of the stirring of the Holy Spirit within us. The vocation to journey to this remote place requires that we leave the scene of pressures and daily life. This same journey replaces it with rolling hills, open country, a glorious coastline and the charm of a Norfolk village of brick, flint and pantile. When pilgrims speak of the peace they have found in Walsingham, this physical and material context provides an environment in which we are perhaps a little more likely to be receptive to the presence of the omnipresent God.

The essays in this section direct our attention to the social dimension of our faith. Stephen Cottrell outlines this as evangelism. His identification of a Marian dynamic in evangelism offers us a kind of ontology of pilgrimage; the pilgrim is the witness, the message, the sign of God's grace, while at the same time being the recipient of all that.

This activity is not necessarily an easy one. I shall never forget the elderly pilgrim in a wheelchair who travels with his wife to Walsingham two or three times each year on public transport. 'That journey,' he told me, 'is my stations of the cross.'

It is by the power of the Holy Spirit that this work is transformed into witness, and transforms us in the undertaking of it. As a reaching out for God it can also be a reaching out to others in witness. This reaching out may be costly (Mary's piercing sorrow), but as Fr Benson of Cowley wrote, 'we must bear the pain of expansion, for we are stretched, indeed not ultimately on the rack of human torture, but on the glorious being of the Holy Ghost.'

Both Elaine Appelbee and Madeleine Bunting look more

closely at the nature of the society in which this stretching out in witness takes place.

Against the background of her work in Bradford, Elaine Appelbee draws practical comparisons between the experience of motherhood today and the gospel accounts of Mary's role in the early life of her son. In a challenging essay Madeleine Bunting explores the values alongside which this role is considered today, and how our sense of personhood has become confused.

St John's Gospel touches on the significance of persons and places in the scene at the foot of the cross. Entrusted to the beloved disciple, who makes a place for her in his own home, Mary is the one, the only one, who welcomed the Eternal Word when he came to his own. As St Augustine observed, in that unique moment of revelation Mary made a place for him in her heart as much as in her womb.

For today's society Mary is a model of personhood. She lives out the dignified role of a mother, courageously. For women and men she is a sign of hope and justice, her *magnificat* a prophecy of the coming kingdom of her son. Mary is also a person who exemplifies the divine vocation to be, defining her own body as a sacred space in which to be free to explore and embrace the virtues of duty, responsibility and self-sacrifice.

In the quest for how to be human now we have the star to follow of Mary, known by tradition as *stella maris*, star of the sea; a beacon of hope for all who are lost in the confusions of society today.

Revelation in Action: Word and Stone

At the National Pilgrimage to Walsingham in 1998 the preacher, Canon Peter Atkinson, told the story of a priest who was asked by Bishop Frank Weston to join his mission to Zanzibar: 'The priest was embarrassed and apologetic. "I don't think I should live in Africa", he said. "I didn't ask you to live," replied Frank Weston. "You can glorify God by your death."'

Death and the glorification of God, resurrection and the glorification of the flesh, are themes intertwined with pilgrimage. The Christian pilgrimage begins in the waters of the font, sharing in the death of Christ in order to share his resurrection. This, the beginning of sacramental life, is an uncompromising statement about the value of the material.

As a place devoted to the celebration of the Word made flesh it is not surprising that Walsingham is a place of vivid and tangible images. Here the reality of the life beyond the grave is witnessed to by symbol and action, which declare with confidence everything that a metaphor stands for; 'it is, and is not', knowing that the metaphorical vision is simply a penalty for the limits of our language, mind and vision.

The images presented to the pilgrim at Walsingham are dazzling indeed. This is *and it is not* the Holy House where Mary encountered Gabriel's salutation, built by Richeldis and visited by pilgrims since 1061. This is *and it is not* the House of God and the Gate of Heaven in which we are presented before the throne of grace in company with saints and angels, our sins forgiven, to worship forever, singing, 'Holy, holy, holy, Lord God of Sabaoth.' And so the image list continues.

The point about a place of pilgrimage is that it is a sacred place. We could describe that as a place in which the penalty of the metaphor seems to be suspended and we can exist as though, simply, *this is*. Although, in such a place, we continue to be people who comprise that mixture of spirit and matter, sin and holiness (metaphorical saints), nonetheless we are changed by the momentary experience of being allowed to be different – to be real saints.

The joy of all this is that pilgrims do it quite naturally. It's the longing that emerges from the daily slog of Christian discipleship; a recovery of life on the cusp of heaven.

Four essays in this section consider this material world of metaphor. Michael Reardon and Ian Boxall deal more directly with the business of the revealing of heaven in architecture and in scripture. In both cases the fluidity of thought and vision which they describe lead us into a rich world of devotional celebration, which suggests that in our liturgy the cerebral accumulation of words and self-conscious gestures may yet be only a pallid derivative from a much richer source.

Looking at the place of cathedrals and churches in our society today, Stephen Platten and Timothy Jones continue this theme of bridge-building between sacred and secular, and extension of the metaphor of christian language into the landscape of our towns, cities and countryside.

In *Re-pitching the Tent* Richard Giles offers this quotation from Frederic Debuyst on the nature of a church: 'The Christian church is neither a sacred monument built to express God's glory, nor simple gathering centre for biblical lectures of social proceedings. It is a Paschal meeting-room, a place where the assembled community experiments and exercises the full impact of the Paschal mystery' (p.143).

The paschal mystery is what defines the nature of our pilgrimage: 'Did not our hearts burn within us as he talked to us on the road and explained the scriptures to us?' (Luke 24.32) A place of pilgrimage embraces revelation in stone, glass, word and action, offering access to a distinctive place in which metaphor is suspended and we find ourselves in the company of the risen Lord, recognizing him in the scriptures and the breaking of bread.

Revelation in Art

A recent article about an exhibition of icons offered the following quotation from Albert Rouet, Bishop of Poitiers: 'A harmony between liturgy and the arts depends . . . upon the liturgy's need to signify, evoke, and make present its conversation about the splendour of God.'[1]

Conversation is the social bond of pilgrimage. It is what gave Chaucer and Bunyan the material for their stories. No doubt it's how the three old sinners of Auden's poem registered and shared their grumbles about food, the journey and the loss of home comforts.

Conversation (as distinct from confrontation or debate) is, therefore, an expression of harmony. It underlines the truth that harmony is not a static condition, but a fluid, dynamic relationship, often changing in tone and mood to reflect the situation of those who participate in it.

The description of a work of art as something that facilitates a conversation is, I think, extremely helpful. In particular, it may help us to understand our relationship with a particular statue or icon which is at the centre of a place of pilgrimage. If these works of art (setting aside the question of their sometimes dubious artistic merit) become part of a conversation in which together we speak about the splendour of God, then we can see that they are not the recipients of our worship, but companions in our quest for holiness.

The pilgrimage revelation here is that of unity, often experienced as healing. The religious work of art or object of devotion expresses a conversation between God and some particular part of his creation in a state of glory and perfection. Our conversation through that work of art draws us into the process of redemption and glorification, so that we can see ourselves as integrated into the very same dynamic of redemptive exchange.

The importance of this today is that it meets the needs of a culture which is increasingly less word-based, less confident of definition, and more tentative, dependent on images and what they might evoke. Here also the revelation is that of unity and integration.

For those who are unfamiliar with or afraid of the propositional demands of Christian faith, the artistic and fluid world of the imagination can offer an experience of spiritual reality, which affords them contact with the dispensation of God's love. This does not mean that Christians should substitute for the invitation to rich, deep, explicit and costly faith some vague and subjective exploration of intuitive feeling. But it does suggest that communication happens through a variety of media, and that the visual arts offer wide and attractive access to conversation about the splendour of God.

The three essays in this series present fascinating reflection on this aspect of revelation. David Brown picks up on the use of the artistic imagination as a springboard into theological conversation, while Sara Boss and Catherine Oakes present an historical survey of the art of the cult of the virgin Mary. In picture form the illustrations to these essays reveal what force and vitality is contained within the familiar words, phrases and stories of the Christian faith.

Pilgrimage is itself a work of art. It is God's art of creativity, in which the journey of life offers us the opportunity to be sculpted, defined and enriched until we arrive at the perfection of his children:

> O how glorious and resplendent
> Fragile body shalt thou be,
> When endued with so much beauty,
> Full of health, and strong, and free,
> Full of vigour, full of pleasure
> That shall last eternally.

Conclusion

Auden's three wise men, old sinners, claim to have only the vaguest idea about their purpose and identity. It is, therefore, all the more remarkable that they should throw up everything to follow the star. The discovery of how to be human now is no less crucial 2,000 years later.

The essays which follow are presented with the conviction that the birth of Jesus Christ was the defining moment in human history and the unique revelation of what it means to be human. Mary is the gateway to that revelation, offering the eternal Word a local address. She is essentially a pilgrim, whose openness defines the pilgrim vocation: Say Yes to God.

Note

1. Quoted by Michael Jones-Frank in Art in the Orthodox Tradition, *Church Buildings*, No. 52, July/August 1998.

PART II

Revealed in Doctrine

The Seal of Orthodoxy': Mary and the Heart of Christian Doctrine

Rowan Williams

Granted, it is not always easy these days to say with complete clarity what the centre and focus of 'orthodoxy' are; but the point of having such a concept in the first place is that Christians should be recognizable to each other, that they should be able to talk to each other in the same language, whatever local dialects may spring up. At the deeper level, the assurance that there is such a language at the centre, and that it remains intelligible across some pretty formidable barriers of history and culture, reinforces the sense that Christian discourse continues to wrestle with the same obstinate reality it displays its concern with an abiding truth, rather than just what makes immediate sense in any particular here and now. The idea of orthodoxy, so far from being a tiresome restriction on what we can say, ought to be an opening out on to a perspective always larger than what I, as an individual, or even we as a contemporary community can grasp and cope with. It points us into a new and fuller world whose patterns are determined by the mysterious action of God in our history; and it invites us to find how the patterns of our own lives may be woven in with these and opened up to the full scope of God's loving act.

The idea of orthodoxy, then, is inextricably linked to the idea of holiness. Not (God knows) that right belief makes you holy; 30 seconds' reflection will disabuse you of any such nonsense. But the idea of an orthodox faith makes no sense unless it is about the conditions that make it possible to live a holy life and the criteria by which Christians recognize this or that life as holy. Adhering to orthodoxy is certainly a matter of honouring truth; but truth and life are inseparable in our faith, and doctrinal truth is discovered in our history *as* people discover what newness of life in Christ is. Orthodox teaching is teaching that invokes and evokes (it is better not to say 'describes', as that might suggest too mechanical an operation) the sort of God who makes possible the life that Christians know in the communion of the Holy Spirit. When this newness of life becomes obscured, the energy of doctrinal commitment and the clarity of doctrinal understanding weaken; and when insistence upon exactitude of doctrine as an end in itself obscures the connection with renewed life in Christ, the life of the worshipping community becomes 'thinner' in texture, more and more dependent upon the chances of subjectivity and the shifts of cultural fashion. The great and lasting revivals of Christian spiritual seriousness (the monastic revival of the 12th century, the Reformation, the new religious movements associated with Teresa of Avila or Ignatius Loyola, the Methodist revival in England and Wales, the early days of the ecumenical movement in our century) have all been occasions for the renewal of doctrinal depth and passion for the rediscovery of the dense and vital texture of credal truth. Our contemporary difficulties over some doctrinal issues need to be put into this perspective: if we are bored or uncomprehending about aspects of our doctrinal tradition, it just might be because we have lost certain spiritual skills; and if our worship and spirituality feels shallow and frustrating, we may need to look again at how to restore its grounding in a richer theological language. Chickens and eggs.

But these are very large issues that need more sustained work than a short essay can offer; the salient point is simply to try and answer the question of why we might care at all about locating Mary within a theological schema. It is more than a matter of intellectual tidiness, as I hope will be obvious. But what are the central features of this schema, the faith set out in the Holy Scriptures and Catholic creeds and historic formularies, to use the familiar Anglican phraseology? Briefly: that we believe in a God whose eternal being is constituted by the relation of three distinct and interdependent subsistent realities (a bit misleadingly called 'persons' for short); that one of these realities, one moment or dimension of the eternal relation, is embodied as completely as possible in the entire human life of Jesus of Nazareth, so that the way the eternal 'person' relates to its source is exactly the way the earthly Jesus relates to this source (as Son to Father or, more abstractly, as mind itself to active intelligence or, more metaphorically, as stream to spring); and that through this embodiment of the eternal Son or Word, the third 'moment' in the divine life becomes newly active in the world, bringing to life in those who unite themselves to Jesus Christ a relation like his to his divine source, so that we too, in dependence upon him, can pray, 'Abba, Father'. This process of growth in the Spirit is bound up with the symbolic actions Christians perform in the belief that these actions will open us up more and more fully, body and spirit, to the power of renewal; the shape of Christ's life becomes naturalized in us through the sacraments – which are always the Spirit's work before they are our activity.

Now, pivotal in all this is the second point in the schema, the entry of God the Word into our world as a concrete, historical agent. The eternal action of God streaming out from the eternal source and reflecting back to it an eternal glory and love, the action which theology calls the generation of the Son from the Father and the Son's eternal self-offering of love to the Father – this is translated into human terms: it becomes not simply an eternal truth about God but a series of events in our world. The theology of the early centuries wrestled painfully and at enormous length with how to say all this without making Jesus either more or less than human as we are human, and without ascribing to God a process of change that would compromise God's completely self-subsistent life. (God doesn't need us in order to be God, and God doesn't belong inside a system of actions and reactions, since he is pure activity in himself.) The precariously balanced statement of the Council of Chalcedon in 451 insisted that Christ be spoken of as *complete* in respect of both humanity and divinity; the theology of both East and West in the centuries that followed spelled out further how this could be said without contradiction and without dehumanizing Jesus. If Mary belongs at the heart of such a doctrinal schema, then, it must be because something about her involvement in the human

translation of divine relations illuminates and secures the sense of
that double completeness that the Council defined. If this can be
teased out, we may understand why a proper theological
evaluation of Mary is a crucial part of expounding the truth about
God in Christ as the orthodox faith receives it.

If we begin to reflect upon Mary's relation to the complete
humanity of Jesus, there are some very obvious leads to follow.
Humanity exists in time and growth, and so it always has in it
elements of dependence. We don't all at once turn into the people we're going to be and, in the interval, we need the input of
others to become ourselves. Clearly then, for Jesus to become
himself, he needed other human beings 'making him human',
contributing their identity to the making of his identity. Jesus is
the Word Incarnate only as a human being in a *context*; for him
to be uniquely the Word of God in the human world, a range of
conditions in that human world must be there. He is only the
Word Incarnate as a Jew, for instance – as someone who knows
God through the inheritance of *this* unique history of faith and
suffering and exile and hope; as someone already living in a
covenant relationship with God. Or again, from a different
perspective, he is only the Word Incarnate with his disciples, as
the focus of a community he shapes. He is himself *as* the one
followed, heard, received (and betrayed) by the Twelve. Here is
Austin Farrer on the subject, memorable as always:

> Humanity is a social fact: we need other men, to be human
> ourselves. What is our mind, but a dialogue with the thought
> of our contemporaries or predecessors? And what is our
> moral being, but a complex of relationships? ... Have you
> reflected that Jesus was that Jesus because of Mary and Joseph
> and the village rabbi, a man to us unknown: above all because
> of the disciples to whom he gave himself and the poor people
> to whose need he ministered? But for these people, he would
> have been another Jesus. To be a man, he must have them,
> and to continue a man (as he still indeed is) he must retain
> them.

> (*A Celebration of Faith*, pp.89–90)

Farrer mentions Mary and Joseph; and it should be clear that those *primary* relations that shape our human character – relations with parents – are of exceptional importance. What Jesus, humanly speaking, grew up into was made possible by his closest human contacts; so that what he is able to give God through his human will and understanding is what is given to his developing humanity by those who first nurture him. If Jesus is able to live in a way that means that all his dealings are, without obstacle, open to God, this must (in the ordinary processes of human development) be enabled by what is given to him by the first human other he encounters. And that first human other is Mary. At the foundation of Jesus' historical humanity lie his relations with his parents but, more particularly, with Mary; hers is the first human face he will in any real sense be aware of. What he sees there is crucial to how he sees God.

If we ignore Mary at this point, if we shrug our shoulders and say that it doesn't much matter what sort of person Mary was, we deny the real humanity of Our Lord, a humanity to which other humanities necessarily contribute. There was once a prevailing style of piety and theology so nervous of saying anything about the human development of Christ, for fear of reducing him to a mere fallible mortal, that it ended up with a Jesus so devoid of human psychological depth as to sound like an automaton. I hope we have got a bit beyond that (though we need to be beware of the opposite peril of blithely assuming we can speculate about the details of Jesus' psychology so as to present him as the prototype of the well-integrated modern subject; if anything, I find this even more depressing . . .); and if we have, then we need simply to acknowledge that Jesus *learned* how to be human. If the humanity he learned was exceptional, the conditions of that learning must have been in some way exceptional. And Mary must be at the centre of that exceptional situation.

I am cautions about rushing to conclusions concerning Mary's preservation from all sin and too readily endorsing the doctrine of her immaculate conception (a distinctively Western teaching with a controverted history, depending heavily on one specific view of original sin); but the instinct behind the doctrine seems to me intelligible enough. Mary so lives in relation to God and others – including her son – that she makes her son uniquely free for God and for others. Her *own* freedom, her own holiness, is part of how God becomes human, human in the real time of the human world, the time in which we grow and learn. We must also say something very similar about all that stands behind Mary, picking up the language of some of our hymnody about Mary as 'daughter of Israel', the one in whom the convenantal calling of God's people comes to fulfilment. *She* is who she is as a Jew – and as a peasant in an occupied country, a woman speaking for those poor and hungry whose voice is raised in the 'Magnificat'. That human reality of poverty and exclusion is also part of what makes Mary Mary – and so of what makes Jesus Jesus. But in all this, the mystery and uncertainty of human freedom is still at work (which is one reason for my caution over the immaculate conception): God brings about his purpose of incarnation by that completely obscure weaving together of his will and human wills that makes way for him in this world of contingency. The role of Mary is not, then, just the free consent to the angel's message at the Annunciation; it is all the diverse ways in which her freedom makes room for God, throughout her life, in such a way that this freedom makes possible the humanity of her son. And it is this freedom in turn, developing through the circumstances of being a Jew and a person of no social or political weight, and a member of a subject people, that so works for God; behind Mary's life is the chaos of human freedom for good and evil that produces both Jewish faithfulness and the sins of aggression, war and occupation. In all this, to borrow Kant's famous dictum, God writes straight with crooked lines.

Taking Jesus' historical humanity seriously, then, obliges us to take Mary seriously. But all that has been said so far doesn't quite take us to the heart of the mystery. It *could* be expressed just by saying that Mary is an extremely marked case of all the relational factors that make Jesus who he is. And it could be misunderstood as suggesting that Mary makes possible a humanity of such high quality that we call it divine – which is emphatically *not* what the orthodox doctrine is claiming! We believe that Christ's entire human existence, from the moment of conception is the presence, action and communication of God. Jesus doesn't become so exceptionally holy by the processes of his human learning and discovering that he is promoted to Godhead. Mary doesn't make Jesus God by being a superlatively good mother. The theological mystery here is that Jesus really does grow and learn as a human being; yet that maturation is a constant bringing to light, bringing to particular life, something that is *already* real at the centre of his being, that is more than just a human psyche – the given, abiding presence of God the Word, the real relation of divine love to divine love that is eternal in heaven. There it is at the root of his identity; all he does and experiences as a human subject will be the out-working and translating of this reality, this divine filiation. Mary does not enable the Word to be God, or Jesus to become divine; she enables a humanity in which there is no obstacle for the divine to be active and self-expressive.

This point is made in a rather different way by an American Protestant theologian writing about the belief in Jesus' virginal conception. It is a belief, he says, that expresses the Christian's refusal to accept

> that the life of Jesus is ultimately subject to any other life . . . With the Resurrection the proclamation is that all things are now subject to his hands, and the birth as well as the passion and death of Jesus are now seen in this light. Here is said to be the one birth and death of a human subject to which all other human births and deaths are subject.
>
> (Christopher Morse, *Not Every Spirit. A Dogmatics of Christian Disbelief*, p.152).

The entire event of Jesus' earthly life expresses the total freedom of God, and the affirmation of God's freedom at work in the very conception of Jesus makes the point dramatically. As Morse goes on to say, it also underlines our belief that the working of the Holy Spirit is not accessible to the documentations of human history. The *fact* of Jesus as the one human life that overcomes death and determines the new limits of human existence must not depend on any process that we can observe or analyse. It is, in the terms already used, the expression of a relational reality of divine love that is always there before us.

Morse does not have much to say specifically about Mary; but the implication of what he says is fairly clear as we turn back to consider again the character of Mary's free response to God. I said a little while ago that her role was more than that of freely consenting to the angel, but was something sustained in all her life. But we had better not forget what the assent to the angel means: there is a specific act in which she receives into herself a reality quite independent of her. She is open to the action of God the Word to so profoundly that 'what is to be born of her', in the Lucan phrase, will be wholly suffused with that action and that life which lives in eternity with the Father. Her continuing discipleship in her own life and death is central to Jesus being humanly what he was (and is), to Jesus being a human personality with the freedom to allow God to speak in all his acts and words. But the God who speaks in Jesus is one who has already bound himself to that human life in the unparalleled closeness of the relationship theologians call the hypostatic union – the relationship that constitutes God the Word the foundation of the specific existence of Jesus in the first place. Mary's nurturing love, however deep and faithful, could of itself do no more than foster another life of extraordinary human holiness; but the incarnation means more than this. The life that is born of Mary is a life of unique potential from the moment of conception because it is the life that is directly sustained by the Word, the life taken by the divine Son in order to create in the human world a perfect enactment of the eternal relationship of the second to the first person of the Trinity which, in turn, is made accessible to human beings by the gift of the Spirit. In brief, Mary receives the creative act of the Word before her work begins of the formation of this human identity over time. The paradoxes of grace and freedom are, of course, especially acute here: the interweaving of the sovereign freedom of God, of the contingent freedom of Mary in relation to God, and of the freedom of Jesus, shaped by the contingencies of his mother's responses to God and by all the rest of the changes and chances of the history into which he comes – all this defies tidy statement. To speak of the 'miracle' of incarnation is not primarily to identify a break in the natural order, but to point to the utterly contingent and free, yet utterly congruent and 'necessary' coming together of these different orders of liberty.

But I think we can and must go a little further here. Mary receives the Word of God, according to Scripture, simply by saying yes to God's promise that she will bear a son. Her assent is an assent to *nothing but* the gift of God's act as the foundation for the new life she will carry in her womb. The virginal conception has become a controversial matter these days, and few seem interested in defending it in strictly theological terms; I suspect this is a failure of nerve or imagination. The affirmation that Jesus comes to be in the world by the pure gift of God entails that Mary has to say yes to God without any worldly support or guarantee; she has to exercise a wholly 'dark' faith, believing the promise of God's gift without anything to support or interpret it ('How can this be?'). We lose something of great significance if we regard the narratives of the virginal conception as an embarrassing extra to the 'real' doctrine of the incarnation. I don't say that belief in the incarnation is not possible without belief in the virginal conception, or that stringent tests should be applied to ensure that all Christian pastors and teachers purport to believe it; only that at the very least we need to wonder whether there are aspects of the full richness of the doctrine that can only be explored by taking seriously these stories. J.N. Figgis, in an article on 'Modernism versus Modernity' written in 1913/1914 and published as an appendix to *The Fellowship of the Mystery*, describes movingly his rediscovery of belief in the virginal conception over many years.

Freedom ... was seen to involve far more than had been thought. That notion of development which made miracles impossible was seen to be mechanical; the immanental philosophy was seen to be, if pushed to the extreme, a Pantheism identifying God and the World. So the glorious liberty of the children of God seemed given; and all the world grew younger day by day, as it does still'. (p.295).

Something about the freedom of God and the freedom of human beings seems to be encoded here in this belief; something too, I have proposed, about Mary's reception in darkness of the Word's full action, which has things to say to all believers about receiving the Word and the cost of it.

The doctrine of the incarnation states that there is no moment of Jesus' life when he is not the Word incarnate; it also states that he is not Word incarnate in virtue of an overruling of human liberty – his or anyone else's – and that the presence of divine action in his action is pure gift, not a reward for outstanding holiness, and thus present before his active life begins. What kind of event could hold or express all this? The narrative of the virginal conception suggests that the answer is this: the absolute welcome of the Creator by a creature in the darkness of a totally unsupported faith, such that the creative freedom of God the Word acts to establish an identity that rests on grace alone, the new life that is Jesus, 'allowed' to exist by Mary's free assent to the angel, nurtured into actual historical life by Mary's free exercise of holiness.

Critical issues about the gospel story remain; so too does the legitimate anxiety that the unique mode of conception somehow detracts from the integral humanity of Jesus. On the former, I can say no more than that these questions are not going to be soluble by historical investigation, and that no amount of apologetic will deliver proof positive of the claim about Mary's virginity. Sara Maitland observes acidly in her delightful book *A Big-Enough God* (p.140), that part of our problem here is a refusal to read imaginatively. She reports a conversation with a priest about the foundations of belief in the virginal conception: 'He said, not unreasonably, that I was cheating. I said I was being imaginative. He said that imagination only distorted the text. I said that they were imaginative texts to start with, so how could imagination distort them?' What if – the question seems to be – the only way of saying certain things really *is* this story? What if the only way of enacting the mystery was the unimaginable event of grace to which it points? What if? This is in fact how the doctrine of the incarnation is related to us in our foundational texts; what if this is how we also must continue to relate it, whatever uncertainties will always surround its proveable foundation in history? If we do so relate it, it seems that insight follows; which may make it worth relating. The idea that there might be a serious theological alternative that captured the same significant complex of concerns would need a good deal of argument before it looked to be worth accepting. Austin Farrer discusses just this possibility in a correspondence, part of which was published by his biographer in 1985 (*A Hawk Among Sparrows: A Biography of Austin Farrer*, by Philip Curtis pp. 242–4). Farrer's correspondent had suggested that Jesus was born in the 'ordinary' course of nature, but that the intercourse of Mary and Joseph took place when both were ecstatically inspired by the Spirit. This would allow the special character of the event to be comparable to the transfiguration – a glorifying, not a bypassing of the processes of the physical world. Farrer does not believe that anything significant is contributed by such a suggestion: it may well be possible to hold an orthodox faith about the incarnation without the virginal conception, but this particular proposal falls between two stools. Farrer's implicit conclusion is, I think, that if we are going to ascribe any special character to Jesus' conception, no modern suggestion is going to make life any easier for the believer than it would be in the light of the actual canonical narrative. This seems to me correct; once the principle of a real supranatural initiative is granted (even in response to the joint spiritual openness of Mary and Joseph), the main point is conceded.

What of the objection that belief in the virginal conception fatally compromises the true or full humanity of Christ? This becomes a problem if we assume that having a really human history must involve being conceived according to the natural generative process. It isn't completely clear that this has to be granted. If Jesus is *perceived* as human, enters into the lives of other human beings as human, shares fully what a human psychology and physiology are open to, including pain, subjective doubt or uncertainty and ignorance about contingent matters of fact, and exists as an embodied person whose corporeal reality is exactly the same in character as our own, what does the natural generative process add to a claim that Jesus shares our nature in every respect of significance? It is obviously impossible for Jesus to share every *possible* human condition (old age, parenthood, blindness and so on): the difficult question is whether sharing the characteristic of having been born as a result of sexual intercourse, or at least (with modern biotechnology suggesting a refinement of this) of the fertilization of an ovum by sperm provided by a male, is essential to any claim about sharing human nature. Theology has traditionally responded by distinguishing between the 'what' of Jesus' humanity and the 'how' of its coming-to-be, arguing (with Maximus the Confessor) that the answer to the former does not foreclose the answer to the latter – not least on the interesting ground that in the trinitarian life Father, Son and Spirit have different modes of origination, yet are identical in nature. Certainly no claim has ever seriously been entertained that the origin of Jesus' historical existence lay in any other event than the fertilizing of an ovum; notions of a kind of disembodied passage through Mary, bypassing the natural process entirely, did not find favour in the early Church. The objection would need to argue conclusively that virginal conception necessarily represented a deficiency in the concrete humanity such as to vitiate any claim for Christ's solidarity with us. If that claim still holds in every respect affecting the existence of Jesus as a distinct human subject, if, that is, it is still a claim that from the moment of conception Jesus is unequivocally on the same footing as we are, yet also wholly transparent to the life of God the Word, I don't think the objection can be conclusive. To borrow the language of patristic theology again, every aspect of human existence that needs to be touched, healed and transfigured by the incarnation is included in what we say about the existence of Jesus as a distinct being whose life begins at conception; and this is not necessarily affected by how we settle the question of the mode of the conception.

I see no quick end to the debate on the virginal conception as an issue in the critical study of the gospel narratives. My goal here has been simply to look at what those narratives might suggest for our understanding of what newness of life in Christ involves. The chief point is that, in addition to the obvious truth that Mary must have a central and crucial role in opening the way for Jesus to be humanly who he is, Mary also embodies a crucial truth about our response to God in Christ. As already stated, she says yes to the living and eternal reality of God's Word in the absence of any worldly assurance or foundation. And in the life in Christ, this is the point to which, in some way or another, we are all drawn – the point of meeting God *as* God and for God's sake, with all our worldly supports taken away and the eyes of understanding darkened. When Mary says yes to the angel, she says yes to God as God – not as one who stands in a system of causes and results, but as the wholly free and wholly mysterious action that is at work in every moment of the universe's existence, and so as the one who can be captured by no identification with any one aspect of the world. Mary's unimaginably complete yes to God as God is what makes possible the action of God as God within the confines of the natural and historical world in a uniquely direct way – as the animating, activating source of a human individual, created by an act of drastic new beginning, by pure divine gift. And all this, not as a violent intrusion into the fabric of created reality, but by the supreme exercise of the highest human freedom, the freedom to empty oneself before the presence of Divine love.

Of course, we learn God from one another; the possibilities of understanding God that mould our faith are bound in with our context – which is why we can speak of Mary as daughter of Israel, and, in turn, of Mary shaping the human faith of Jesus as it evolves in an historical story. But what we learn draws us to a fuller and infinitely harder knowledge of God: the knowledge of the sheer liberty of God's transcendence, God's *glory*, which happens when all expectations, all argument and evidence, all props for faith give way to an encounter in nakedness and darkness. Many spiritual writers have compared the generation of the Word in the human spirit in darkness and unknowing with the conception of Christ in the womb of Mary. When the human self is still, dispossessed and unprotected by image or idea, the Word is free to enter. If the Word is literally and materially born from Mary's consent to 'God as God', we may well reflect not simply on her faith but on the utter darkness of that faith, so complete is her will to say yes to nothing but God.

To put side by side Mary's role as standing for the whole pattern of human dependence that shapes Jesus' identity, and Mary's darkness of self-giving faith, is to be reminded of the two dimensions of human sanctity as revealed in her and her son. There is no holiness without dependence, without taking on and assenting to the complex world that makes me who I am; no holiness for an individual seeking simple autonomy. Accepting that involves me in a profound letting-go of one of the most powerful forces opposing my healing – the illusion of my self-sufficiency. As I learn through my human relationships to assent to this letting-go, I am being prepared for the central and basic act of letting-go which is my nakedness before God as God. The highest act of our freedom becomes this nakedness. This is why St John of the Cross can say that Jesus, immobilized on the cross, surrendered totally to the Father, is more active than at any other point in his incarnate life. This is why we say that Mary's yes to the annunciation is the supreme moment of human welcome to the actuality of God in the form of the new creation that is Jesus, a welcome wholly independent of assurance, proof and ground. 'How can this be?' asks Mary; the answer is simply that the power of the Most High will do what is promised.

As we look at the relation of Mary and her son, we may understand just a little more of what God asks of us if we are willing to take seriously the pattern of orthodox faith we have received. Because of Christ, we are both summoned and enabled to walk with Christ to his cross and resurrection, to the nakedness of faith in the face of the nakedness of God's reality. The gradual formation in us of the likeness of Christ by the communion of believers and the whole mysterious complex of human lives and influences around, is moving us towards this end: the birth, the painful birth, of the eternal Word which comes when we are dispossessed enough to welcome God without reserve and without reassurance. If in some measure we are made free for this, we enter into the new life in which the divine energy lives freely in us: the saint's habitual experience of grace is an analogue, no more, but no less, of the perfect union of the divine and the human in Jesus. This is the orthodox faith; and it finds its lifeblood in the mystery summed up in Mary's yes, in her love-in-darkness. Orthodoxy's lifeblood is here, just as – literally – Christ's lifeblood begins here.

References

P. Curtis, *A Hawk Among Sparrows: A Biography of Austin Farrer*, London, SPCK 1985.
A. Farrer, *A Celebration of Faith: Communications, Mostly to Students*, London, Hodder 1970.
J. N. Figgis, *The Fellowship of the Mystery*, London, Longmans 1914.
S. Maitland, *A Big-Enough God: Artful Theology*, London, Mowbray 1995.
C. Morse, *Not Every Spirit. A Dogmatics of Christian Disbelief*, Valley Forge, PA, 1994.

PART III

Revealed in Society

Contemporary Issues for a Holy Family

Elaine Appelbee

To reflect on the experience of the Holy Family and its place in the life of the Church today is a timely exercise. The experience of contemporary family life is attracting a great deal of religious, political and public attention, most of which is angst-ridden. What, one might ask, have the slender descriptions of the family life of Jesus of Nazareth to say to contemporary Britain about the state of its familial life 2,000 years down the line?

The first thing which we might draw from these stories is the fact that 'holy families' are likely to be ordinary families: ordinary families which accept complexity and challenge in daily life as a given and embrace it. But is there such a thing as an 'ordinary' or 'normal' family? Every 'ordinary' family will have the extra-ordinary to deal with at some stage of its development. Whenever two or more people live together in an intimate relationship anything can, and usually does, happen. So the fact that God chose a seemingly ordinary, normal young girl in an ordinary, normal family to achieve his extraordinary purposes should not strike us as odd. The whole point about the incarnation was to experience and engage with human life in all its manifestations.

While the circumstances in which the Virgin Mary conceived Jesus were extraordinary, and the experience of a young girl, pregnant outside wedlock might have been less common then than now, the ambivalent feelings and fears which must have assailed Mary would be wholly recognizable by many pregnant young women today.

The disapproval which Mary would have been anticipating, the risk of being disowned by her family and abandoned to a future which must not have borne thinking about, not to mention the wrath of her betrothed, would all be recognizable to many young women today. It is easy to think that in our society there is an easy acceptance of out-of-wedlock pregnancy, with a welfare state ready to provide for every need and parents and friends happy to approve and support. However, today's reality

can be just as horrendous as the one Mary might have faced, had
not angels intervened.

Pamela was pregnant, 17 years old and thrown out by her
family. She had no contact with her boyfriend, and was placed in
a cold flat with few belongings in a bleak little estate with no
name. She had no friends, no neighbours whom she could trust
and a tiny income from Social Security. Mary and Pamela would
have had no problem in swapping experiences! And they could
have gone on understanding each others' situation through Mary
and Joseph's subsequent escape into Egypt, with few resources,
dependent on the support and help of strangers. So could the
many families in Britain who have come to this country seeking
asylum as refugees. With them Mary and Joseph would have
understood the fear and the difference made to one's security by
the warmth or coldness of the hospitality offered. The glibness
with which politicians of all parties talk about young, single
pregnant girls or asylum seekers as self-seeking scroungers,
deliberately choosing to place themselves in their various predica-
ments in order to wrest resources from an over-generous welfare
state beggars belief, and denies the reality of the majority of
people in circumstances such as these.

There has been some debate recently about the social and
economic status of the Holy Family. Some argue that, in fact, the
Holy Family was the historical equivalent of our middle class and
that it is wrong to perceive them as 'poor'. This view is challenged
by some who provide evidence to suggest that the Holy Family
were most likely to have been peasant farmers, with a small
holding whose income had to be supplemented by other earn-
ings, hence the need for Joseph to use his skills as a carpenter. So
whilst the family were not close to destitution, which would have
been the plight of the 'poor' in those days, they were by no means
to be classed with the wealthy. Perhaps traditional working class
would be closest to our modern understanding.

We should dwell on the economic status of the Holy Family
because economics plays a crucial role in determining the shape
of families, and the relationships within them. For the past 20
years we have been living though major economic, technological
and social change, tantamount to a new industrial revolution.

The effects of these changes on traditional working-class communities and the families within them can be observed on an outer estate and in the inner city of Bradford. The effects have been profound.

Whilst we can focus on what is happening in such communities because the effects are seen there most starkly, it is important to understand that these changes are also impacting on more affluent communities, but the effects there are less obvious because people are more likely to have access the resources which cushion the impact. The effects on white and minority ethnic working-class communities have been profound. Bradford's recent history has mirrored the history of the other great northern manufacturing cities, which have seen their economic bases devastated by the collapse of the traditional industries upon which those cities were founded. The departure of 'work' from 'working-class' communities had affected not only the local economy, but also the culture of family and society.

The cultural glue, which gives meaning to every area of life, bonding people to one another, is rapidly dissolving. An example of this is what has happened to the socialization of young men in such communities. Work provided an important support to parents as their teenage boys grew to be men. It provided the means by which young, daft boys became sensible young men to whom young women were prepared to commit themselves. The workplace provided older men and an hierarchy through which boys learnt skills, discipline and self-control. When the paid work disappeared, so did the contribution it made to this process and nothing had filled that void. The result is that daft young boys grow into daft and sometimes dangerous young men, whom young women dare not live with. The young women have a sexual relationship, and even a parenting relationship, with their boyfriends, but may feel it wiser to live separately, where the women can be in control.

Poverty has increased dramatically in these communities. Increased poverty is a by-product of this economic and social change and is a complex issue. It is multi-stranded; a plait of poverties and disadvantage, which combine to form a rope strong

enough to strangle the people caught up in it. There are five
strands to this plait:

1. Economic poverty. Poverty is not simply about money but,
   obviously, a lack of money is the pivot.
2. Poverty of environment, including a lack of sense of personal
   safety, even within one's home.
3. Poverty of choice. This includes diet, education, housing and
   other major things, but also small things like the brand of
   coffee one would like to drink.
4. Poverty of opportunity, which leads to a poverty of hope.
5. Poverty of power. A sense of hopelessness is fed by powerless-
   ness. People feel that they cannot affect those in power and feel
   excluded from democracy. There are no votes in poverty.
   Voiceless, choiceless and powerless, the poor are at the mercy
   of changing political goalposts.

Poverty causes an impact at every level – physical, psychological
and social. At its starkest, poverty causes early death. Infant
mortality rates are higher and early deaths in adults from cancer,
heart disease and other causes is rife. This applies to relative as
well as absolute poverty.

On a psychological level the key disabling effect of poverty is
to create a lack of self-esteem. Negative messages beamed directly
into people's homes by the media stereotype and scapegoat the
poor. In the 1930s, where it was clearer that economic recession
and not personal failure accounted for unemployment, and
people lived within more supportive, cohesive communities, the
depressive effects of poverty were mitigated. For parents, the
failure to provide all that they want to for their children leads to
feelings of guilt.

Poverty is isolating. There are very few social activities which
do not involve money in some way or another. Poverty means less
opportunity to make friends. Living on benefits restricts
mobility. Poverty within communities increases the risk of crime,
so that neighbours become a source of suspicion rather than a
source of friendship and support.

Families and their organization have begun to adapt to

changes in society. The increasing privatization of the nuclear family weakens links between the extended family and the wider community. All sorts of reasons are given for this, such as increased mobility, leisure and entertainment which can be provided literally 'in-house', and increased access to cars so that people have even less opportunity for casual contact.

The maelstrom of economic and technological change which has contributed to the fracture of families, communities and culture has, as a consequence, severely undermined people's confidence to parent, particularly in white working-class communities. The traditional ways of learning parenting skills by observation and experience, within a confident culture with its own norms and expectations of what makes for good child care, transmitted by the extended family and friendship networks, are less available. There are undermining effects on parenting skills also being experienced in minority ethnic communities.

In the 1930s if you provided a roof, food and affection for your children that was good enough. Now we know a great deal more about the sorts of circumstances that enable children to thrive and reach their potential. These new, and often unrealistic expectations, which are predicated on the assumption that people have easy access to the information available and the means to act on what they read, are the standards by which parents are measured. This is also so for middle-class parents who turn naturally to written information, but even for them a book can be cold comfort in the middle of the night with a sick child. For many others, struggling to cope with poverty and a difficult environment, the effect of this has been to undermine people's confidence in their ability to parent. The withdrawal of supports for parents from the community arena is telling.

Teenagers might be thought to be a phenomenon of late-20th-century Western society, but look at the Gospel of Luke, 2: 41–52. You will remember the story of the Holy Family's trip to Jerusalem. It is a description of fairly typical teenage behaviour by Jesus, obsessed with his own concerns, thoughtless about the trouble he might cause and unable to understand what all the fuss is about, when Mary and Joseph finally track him down. And their inability to appreciate fully the theological significance of his action! The line at the end of the story, 'he then went down with them and came to Nazareth and lived under their authority', makes this writer smile as she visualizes the row there must have been on the way home. Teenage discovery learning!

One of the reasons why it took so long for Mary and Joseph to discover that Jesus was missing was not because they were irresponsible parents, uncaring about where he was and what he might be getting up to, but because parenting was shared within a wider household and community. Parents were not left to stand on their own two feet and bring up their children in isolation, without help and support. The adults making up the party travelling to Jerusalem would have shared responsibility for all the children in the group, watching out for them.

In our society adults are losing the confidence to befriend, aid or admonish children and young people in the public space (i.e. outside home and school). It is as if children and young people have been privatized. We are told that they are the responsibility only of their parents or teachers. But that third arena 'out there' in the community has also been an important place where children have learnt social skills and how to relate to others. Public space is particularly important for young people as they move out of the home environment. Adults are afraid to intervene and act as adults, which can lead in the worst cases to estates being held to ransom by their children. If young people, away from their parents, receive no feedback from adults in the community about their behaviour, then it is hardly surprising that the situation gets out of control.

Of course there are good reasons for this lack of confidence – unrelated adults and children, particularly within urban communities, are less likely to know each other by name. There is the fear of adults that they may be accused of abusing or molesting a child, or fear of retribution because of the isolated but sensational stories which appear in the press from time to time. So adults who might once have augmented the parenting role, have withdrawn, allowing the generations to become increasingly suspicious and intolerant of each other, and leaving parents without the necessary additional supports which they need to fulfil their role.

A consequence of all this is a serious fracture which is developing between the generations, as well as within communities. Children learn through campaigns such as 'Stranger Danger' to be suspicious of adults whom they do not know. Yet all the evidence is that where there is abuse, it is likely to be committed by adults whom children do know. At the other end of the scale, if older people see a group of teenagers approaching them they are fearful of what might happen. Teenagers feel this suspicion, which confuses them and leads to resentments.

This is painting a very gloomy picture – but then for many families in struggling communities life is desperately gloomy, as a comment from a Bradford housing estate illustrates: 'We feel that for 90 percent of families on the estate, life is rough. They are demoralized, afraid, lonely, depressed, without hope and often humiliated by their circumstances. Young or old it makes no difference. For many, life is hard and sad.'

So we come to the ministry which Jesus went on to develop, after the kick-start given by his mother at the wedding at Cana. A ministry which engaged with the wider society was focused on the healing of relationships between God and between people; which offered new possibilities for how people organized to live together and which affected both family and community.

If we have concerns about the ways in which contemporary families appear to operate, then we need to address the wider influences which inform their organization and behaviour. The way in which we live together as a society, the kind of community which this organization spawns, is critical for the health and well-being of the family groups within it.

The notion of a Holy Family includes us, the Church, as a Holy Family. What is the task for us in our bit of history, following the example of the adult Jesus? In this ministry of salvific love, healing and reconciliation began with those who were most marginalized and suffering the greatest pain, and it focused on the relationships between them and the rest of society.

Using this model the urgent task for the Church in our society is helping in the reconstruction of our fractured communities, which will, in turn, strengthen the families within them. Using Bradford as an example it is possible to describe some action which is being developed there. In terms of trying to tackle the many challenges facing cities like Bradford, there have been a plethora of initiatives undertaken by the major institutions and agencies with varying degrees of success. However, it has become clear that if sustained, positive change in to occur then people from local communities need to be involved in the thinking and planning, otherwise very little will happen or change.

It was into this arena that the churches stepped in 1993, when the ecumenical Bradford Metropolitan Faith in the City Forum undertook a project called 'Powerful Whispers'. This project brought together the key decision-makers within the Metropolitan District and some of the people living in four of the most disadvantaged areas of the District. The aim was to hear directly from the people concerned, including local professionals, about how life is experienced by them; to demonstrate that even in hard-pressed communities there were people with ideas who would be fitting partners for the work of regenerating the District; and to help create a public debate about the future of Bradford. Many of the speakers were women, because it is most often women who are willing to engage in building community. A key reason appears to be that they are most willing to take risks for the sake of their children. Despite the fact that they might be scared to death to walk through the doors of a community centre, nonetheless they are prepared to take the risk because their children need the company of other children at the local parent and toddler group, for instance.

Four urban 'hearings' were held and out of these came a common agenda of concerns – poverty, crime, young people, race, culture and religion, consultation and decision-making and housing. The hearings had a profound effect on the decision-makers who had sat for eight hours listening silently. One of the most powerful effects was to remind everyone concerned that we do share a common humanity and inhabit the same world. One of the 'hearers' said: 'I never realized that people want the same kinds of things as me.' Another remarked that it was true that resources are scarce but he was left wondering whether the right people were being listened to when decisions were made about how those resources should be allocated.

Those hearings help us come to a new understanding of the Magnificat. Sometimes our initial understanding is that complete revolution is implicit in the text. The only problem with such a revolution is that those who had previously been at the bottom tend to copy the behaviour of the previously powerful, and the unhelpful cycle repeats itself. But through the 'Powerful Whispers' project, perhaps the Magnificat could be read as raising up the lowly and bringing down the mighty to the point where they can speak directly to one another, allowing new relationships to be formed. That may be the real revolution.

Following the hearings, the Forum then went on to listen to the decision-makers talk about how they felt about having the responsibility for trying to solve the problems. It then considered how the project might be built upon.

Out of the six common issues, consultation and decision-making were the surprise. It challenged the official view that the regeneration projects, which had been undertaken in the District, were, bar one exception, 'bottom up'. Furthermore, the damage done to the communal solidarity of the District by the competitive nature of the bidding system in use was palpable, particularly as the decision-making was not transparent. Consequently areas of the District which were not involved in these large 'bids' were left feeling even more marginalized.

On the other hand, the Powerful Whispers process also demonstrated that despite diversity there was a clear common agenda around which the increasingly separated and diverse communities of the District could be reconnected. What was being seen was a plethora of strategies from the top, and at the 'bottom' a great deal of *ad hoc* activity responding directly to needs. For those at the top there was a frustration that nothing appeared to move the District forward in the way that had been hoped, and at the bottom a frustration that nobody was listening. There appeared to be a gap in the middle where the top and the bottom were failing to connect. This connection will not be made without a self-conscious attempt to make it happen. None of the subsequent discussions with the decision-makers led the Forum to believe that they knew how to set about this work. Nor, to be fair, was there any reason why they should.

The report of the Bradford Commission into the Manningham riots reflected this view in a telling paragraph:

The critical political deficiency which we have found [in Bradford] is that there is no adequate process to link the concerns of the responsible members of the public, or those working at the problems 'on the ground', with the means of participating effectively in developing local solutions. We challenge the City to produce at many levels, the leadership and the co-ordination which can channel the strengths of Bradford to deal with the problems we identify in this report.

In the summer of 1997 the Faith in the City Forum came up with an idea for how a piece of work could be constructed to meet the challenge expressed so eloquently in the Commission report. It is called 'The Centenary–Millennium Project (C2M). It aims to bridge this gap. The central idea is a simple one – to encourage as many communities in the District as possible to use the time between the City's Centenary (just ended) and the other side of the Millennium to build local agendas and plans for their communities. This will aim to take community initiatives into a further stage of development where the response will not just be *ad hoc* but, first, would take stock of all the strengths and weaknesses of the community, and then prioritize and plan the response.

In this way every community will have the opportunity to participate and create a forward momentum for themselves. Community planning will happen at an appropriate pace, not driven by funding deadlines, and will put communities in a strong position to bid for funds, from all sorts of sources, in the future. If there is a plethora of community plans, then the criteria can be displayed and those with agreed plans which best fit those criteria can be put forward in a transparent manner and an open debate take place about which is chosen and why, when subsequent Government money does appear.

Every community can act in partnership with institutions to improve the quality of life. It does not always have to depend on waiting for huge screeds of Single Regeneration Budget or other money.

Here is a concrete example of an actual piece of work which

reflects this approach. A small local community centre in the heart of the inner city has been running very successfully for several years. The management of the centre is shared between local people, the local parish church and Social Services, with local people in the majority. The management committee decided it was time to have a community survey to check whether the services and activities currently offered were still relevant to the needs of the community and whether new needs were emerging. A group of volunteers at the centre, all local mothers, participated in this work. They undertook training to discover how to draw up a questionnaire, how to plan the sample, to devise the script and approach the work. In addition, they published their findings and held an open evening for members of the community and founders so that the findings could be verbally and visually presented. None of them had ever done anything like this before. One of them had spent the previous three years learning to read and write, two had suffered life-threatening illness. Two others had been developing skills and confidence through educational courses.

As a result of the community survey a gap in the provision for young people was identified. With a couple of hundred pounds left from a summer trip they started a girls' group, which ran very successfully for several months. Supported by the community worker they put together a bid to the National Lottery Charity Board and succeeded in winning a grant of £190,000 to establish a youth project.

In order to encourage this type of bottom-up audit, planning and action work the churches have brought together a wide-ranging partnership, backed by the major institutions within the District, to set up the C2M project. As well as inviting and resourcing communities to participate in the programme, it will enable three other crucial things to happen.

The first will be to link across the District groups and communities which have common emerging agendas, plans or actions. The purpose of these links will be to share ideas and good practice. C2M has received half a million pounds grant from the Millennium Commission to make such grants to individuals, or two or three people working together on the C2M programme.

These grants will carry a requirement to participate in small Action Learning groups with other recipients. In this way people from very different communities will become connected through common concerns and actions, and from this it is anticipated that people across Bradford District will come to believe that, within diversity, we share a common humanity.

We often find it almost impossible to celebrate the wonderful God-given diversity which exists within our wider society. Perhaps it is because diversity, detached from any understanding that we share common values and concerns, frightens us by highlighting our differences and allowing us to view each other only as aliens. Perhaps when we are confident that we hold some key values and concerns in common, then we can believe that diversity is something to safely celebrate and enjoy.

The second crucial task will be to work with institutions to increase their capacity to partner more effectively with communities. For the previous 40 years local government was confident in its role as the key provider of services for local communities. Whilst the last ten years have seen an erosion of this role, it has only led to an increase in the 'quango' culture and the consolidation of a 'those at the top know best' mentality, despite the occasional rhetoric of community partnership. Expertise has been seen as resting with the professionals. There is a need for a shift in this culture. We must recognize that local communities, no matter how struggling, have the ability to develop the expertise to make a critically important contribution to the development of a mature society.

The third task for C2M is to enable the information and good practice being generated at the grassroots to be gathered and passed on to those who have responsibility, for thinking strategically about services and plans for the District.

Through this project it is hoped to enhance the ability of the citizens of Bradford District and its institutions to dismantle the current barriers of race, class and culture and to learn from each other, as together they take hold of the future – in effect to create a learning District. In this way we begin to reconstruct and strengthen community life and widen the opportunities for participation.

At the end of the 20th century the nature of the forces of change demand a radical reconstruction of the way we organize ourselves as a society. The structures which underpin our society, including community and family, and the roles which they play need to be renegotiated. This is recognized by politicians, hence all the Government reviews, but I am anxious that they should not feel that it is their task to do this work for us! We all need to be involved in that renegotiation. There are no short cuts and again this is a task for us all, not just for politicians. Confidence developed through valued participation is the key ingredient.

A group of young mothers on a large council estate in Bradford described graphically why they could not walk through the large wooden doors of their local church, even when those doors were standing wide open. Whilst they knew that the Church was supposed to be for them, that it was something to do with loving and caring for others, still they did not have the confidence to walk through those doors.

The challenges which we face together in our society could so easily become opportunities if we move from a culture which seeks to blame and scapegoat, into one which acknowledges that recent economic and social change has affected every area of our lives for good and ill, and seeks to redress the price being paid by the most vulnerable. It is our task to enable people to become confident, valued and empowered members of an inclusive society, made up of coherent communities which sustain healthy families.

Mary the Evangelist

Stephen Cottrell

'Doxology is the heart-beat of evangelism'
(Archbishop George Carey)

Mary set out at that time and went as quickly as she could into the hill country to a town in Judah. She went into Zechariah's house and greeted Elizabeth. Now it happened that as soon as Elizabeth heard Mary's greeting, the child leapt in her womb and Elizabeth was filled with the Holy Spirit. She gave a loud cry and said, 'Of all women you are the most blessed, and blessed is the fruit of your womb. Why should I be honoured with a visit from the mother of my Lord? Look, the moment your greeting reached my ears, the child in my womb leapt for joy. Yes, blessed is she who believed that the promise made her by the Lord would be fulfilled.'

And Mary said:

> My soul proclaims the greatness of the Lord,
> and my spirit rejoices in God my Saviour;
> because he has looked upon the humiliation of his servant.
> Yes, from now onwards all generations will call me blessed,
>   for the Almighty has done great things for me.
> Holy is his name,
> and his faithful love extends age after age to those who fear
>   him.
> He has used the power of his arm,
> he has routed the arrogant of heart.
> He has pulled down princes from their thrones and raised
>   the lowly.
> He has filled the hungry with good things, sent the rich
>   away empty.

He has come to the help of Israel his servant, mindful of his faithful love – according to the promise he made to our ancestors – of his mercy to Abraham and to his descendants for ever.

(Luke 1: 39–55)

Most teenage girls know the importance of that little word 'no'. Thank God Mary knew the importance of that little word 'yes'. With her yes to God, his mission of love to the world can at last unfold. Her visit to Elizabeth is the first missionary journey in Christian history. Responding so completely to the message of the angel, she rushes to visit her cousin to share the joy of what God has done in her life, and what God is going to do through the child growing in her womb.

Elizabeth Jennings describes this visit as 'a moving silence through the land', and goes on

> 'And all her journeying was a caressing
> within her mind of secrets to be spoken.
> The simple fact of birth soon overshadowed
> the shadow of the angel. When she came
>   Close to her cousin's house she kept
> Only the message of her happiness.[1]

As with all missionary activity Mary is not acting in her own strength, but giving from the overflow of what she has received. Mary is able to go faithfully to others, because she has received faithfully herself. Her life embodies Jesus' words: 'Give, and there will be gifts for you: a full measure, pressed down, shaken together, and overflowing' (Luke 6:38). She has received – and therefore she has much to give. She gives – and more is added to her.

Her example shows us how to respond and be obedient to the word of God. In her encounter with the angel Gabriel we see a pattern of greeting and response which echoes the whole process of evangelism as good news is shared with others and as we, Christ-bearers to the world today, seek out a response. When the angel first tells Mary of God's promise, Luke tells us she is 'deeply disturbed' (Luke 1:29). This is the quite normal reaction to a dawning awareness that there might be more to life than we had imagined. Mary was in all probability a faithful Jewish girl, obedient to the promises and prohibitions of her faith and culture. Now she is spun off centre by the radical intervention of God in her life. The last thing she would have felt like doing is rejoicing! The situation today is not so different. Although it is expressed in very different ways, people are still obedient to their own values, beliefs and culture. We may speak of moral decline and structural breakdown in our society, but the actual truth is that most people live quiet, dignified and law-abiding lives. They may be aware that there is something more to life – they may indeed have some kind of belief in God – but until something happens to confront them with the scandalous and shattering claims of the Christian faith, it is unlikely that the gospel will much disturb their equilibrium. When this does happen there are many questions. 'How can this be?' says Mary to the angel (Luke 1:34). Surely this is what most of us have cried out when we first glimpsed the majesty of God. We are overwhelmed with astonishment, disbelief, confusion: we are full of searching questions. Faith comes, not through having every question answered, still less every hardship removed – Mary is told that a sword will pierce her heart (Luke 2:35) – but through abandonment to the will of God. Faith comes as a gift in response to our surrender. Freely, though fearfully and tentatively, we say yes to God. This is what is seen in the life of Mary. She places herself at God's disposal. Again and again she points the way to Jesus. Her life is his life; she shares the promise of eternal life with others, because she has received the promise of eternal life from him. 'Let it happen to me as you have said' (Luke 1: 38) are the words that begin the Christian faith; they are about our free response to God's searching love. Only when we have said these words can evangelism begin. They echo the response of Isaiah: 'Here am I, send me' (Isaiah 6:8). They foreshadow the call of the disciples, who leave everything to follow Jesus.

And so Mary rushes to see her cousin Elizabeth; rushes to tell her good news. The response of the angel to her question – how can this be? – was not so much an answer as a promise: 'The Holy Spirit will come upon you, and the power of the Most High will cover you with its shadow. And so the child will be holy and will be called Son of God' (Luke 1:35). Mary is brimming with the Spirit. Through the Holy Spirit Jesus has been formed in her; he takes his flesh from her flesh. This is always the way the Holy Spirit works in the lives of those who believe. We may indeed cry out, how can this be? It seems too amazing that God could make his home in us, but this is the scandalous heart of Christian faith: the God who is everywhere becomes the God who is somewhere. The God who spoke and the universe was, is now a cluster of cells dividing into life in the flood tide of Mary's womb. God has emptied himself of what it is to be God in order to know what it is to be human.

And Elizabeth recognizes in Mary this turning of the axis of eternity: it is from this moment that time will be measured. Mary's surrender to the will of God is the pivot of the ages: 'Blessed is she who believed that the promise made her by the Lord would be fulfilled' (Luke 1:45). Thus it is that as soon as Elizabeth hears Mary's greeting she too is filled with the Holy Spirit and filled with holy joy. So much so that the child in her womb leaps in exultation. It is the first piece of evangelism. Mary bears good news to her cousin.

And as the Holy Spirit ignites In Elizabeth's heart, and as the unborn Baptist turns in the womb towards the unborn Christ, so faith comes to life and Mary sings for joy. The words of her song embrace some of the major themes of the Christian faith. But what is relevant here is that they also provide a pattern for the sharing of faith. The Magnificat is an evangelistic text. It is testimony to all that God has done. It is proclamation of his saving love. By looking at it in some detail I believe we can learn about evangelism.

Mary Rejoices in God's Grace

'You will show me the path of life; in your presence is the fullness of joy. (Psalm 16:11)

My soul proclaims the greatness of the Lord,
and my spirit rejoices in God my Saviour;
because he has looked upon the humiliation of his servant.
Yes, from now onwards all generations will call me blessed,
for the Almighty has done great things for me.

Evangelism is about sharing joyful good news. Jesus says that his
mission is to bring abundant life (John 10:10) But too much
evangelism starts by telling people the bad news that they are lost,
rather than the good news that God is looking for them: that he
promises life in all its fullness. Christian joy is therefore that exultation of the spirit when we find union with God. It is much
more than happiness. Of course there is plenty of delight to be
found in the world around us, and all this is good. We are not
wanting to say that joy in the Lord replaces the joy we find in
daily life. Rather, it is like having enjoyed drinking water from
the tap, we suddenly discover the clear purity of water at its
source. Mary sings of God's greatness because she discovers the
living God as the source of all joy and all life. She does not
exchange the delights of this life for the delights of God, rather
she sees the delights of the world in a new perspective. They are
all part of God's gift; all part of his loving purpose. 'His glory fills
the whole earth' says Isaiah (Isaiah 6:3). It is hard to under-
estimate the shocking audacity of this claim. God is no longer
separate from the world he made. In Christ he comes among us,
revealing in sharp clarity both his otherness – the God who is
emptied in order to share – and his closeness – present in the
womb of Mary, foreshadowed in every particle of creation (see
Romans 1:20). 'The world is charged with the grandeur of God,'
writes Gerard Manley Hopkins.

> It will flame out, like shining from shook foil;
> It gathers to greatness, like the ooze of oil
> Crushed.[2]

When we share the faith with others we should tell of the good
things that God has done in our lives. We should let our praise
flame out, reflecting on the places where we have received God's

healing and restoring grace. We have all known want and sterility in one area of life or another; we all seek that integrity of life where mind and body and spirit find union with each other through union with God. To actively ponder on the ways in which God is achieving this integrity in us will not only come to us as blessing, it will draw us into closer relationship with people around us and to the earth of which we are part. The gospel comes to 'open up rivers on barren heights . . . to turn dry ground into springs of water; to plant the desert with cedar trees, acacias, myrtles and olives' (Isaiah 41:18–19). We should expect this in our life as we say our yes to God. And we should not be embarrassed about sharing our experience of these things with others. The most effective evangelism is the sharing of testimony; and the best testimony is simple good news of the difference that God has made.

People today live fragmented lives. Families do not communicate. We live in fear of our neighbours, trembling behind shut doors and security-barred windows. Everyone is guilty until we find them innocent. Within ourselves we seek improvement of mind, or else try to roll back the ravages of age and death with ever more demanding regimes of diet and exercise. Meanwhile the food we eat is poisoned by the extremities of factory farming as we distort nature to conform to our ever increasing greed. Where there is a search for spiritual truth often it aims to disconnect from life, replacing the hostilities of the world for an empty truce with a non-personal god. Community shrivels. Expectations fade. Postponing death becomes the chief pre-occupation of life. Within this vortex of despair, made worse by the gilded luxury of our enclosure and the numbing paucity of our hopes, the gospel must come as liberation – from self to community; from private to corporate; from fragmented to united. When people experience the gospel as putting life back together again it will be good news. Mary says: 'The Almighty has done great things for me. Holy is his name.' She has been restored to God and therefore she has been restored to herself and to the whole creation. Jesus says, 'The truth will set you free' (John 8:32). But many people today think of the gospel as a snare. They imagine it is just a list of things to believe in, not a way for life. Too much evangelism has proceeded on the basis of persuading people of the truth of Christian faith, rather than bearing witness to the liberation of Christian life. We can learn from Mary a more integrated approach to being Christian, and therefore a more life-affirming approach to evangelism. Faith is a gift. God is the Evangelist. From his grace flow faith and joy. Our evangelism witnesses to his grace and the joyful faith it has wrought in us. And this holy joy, drawing us closer to God and closer to one another, is what every human heart longs for. When people find it, through the example of the lives we lead and by the testimony of the words we share, faith will blossom. Joy is infectious.

Mary Tells of God's Mercy

'I am like a green olive tree in the house of God; I trust in the mercy of God for ever.' (Psalm 5:8)

> Holy is his name,
> and his faithful love extends age after age to those
>   who fear him.

Mary delights that God has found her. He has looked upon her lowliness and raised her up. This is pure gift: the joy she shares flows from the grace she has received. It is for this reason that Mary is held up as a model for the Church: she responds with thankfulness to the free gift of God's love. Her song of joy fulfils the song of Hannah (1 Samuel 2:1–10); who had also experienced God's merciful love. It foreshadows the song of every Christian who finds rest in God's mercy.

The merciful God is always seeking out the lost and offering them the hope of restoration. He looks upon the humiliation of all his servants. He is always raising high the lowly. God's very nature is mercy. In the Old Testament this is closely bound up with the faithfulness of his love. He is merciful because he is loving. He delights over the repentance of one sinner more than the upright lives of the 99 (Luke 15:7). Even the smallest sign of our repentance is sufficient for the outpouring of his grace. Down through the ages Christians have found that if you take one little step towards God, he takes a mighty leap towards you. The Father has only to see the returning prodigal approaching in the distance and he is moved with pity. He runs to meet his son, and before the boy has even had a chance to confess his failure and his sin, the Father clasps him in his arms and kisses him (Luke 15:21).

> Integrity and generosity are marks of the Lord
> for he brings sinners back to the path.
> Judiciously he guides the humble,
> instructing the poor in his way.
> Kindness unfailing and constancy mark all the Lord's paths,
> for those who keep his covenant and his decrees.
>
> (Psalm 25:8–10)

Mary experiences this bountiful mercy in her own life and in the life of her cousin Elizabeth. It gives her assurance that she is loved and reconciled to God.

We need this loving countenance when we speak of sin and forgiveness. Although the first word of the gospel must always be love, we cannot back away from talking about sin. Our hearts are hewn as thrones for God, but we have placed ourselves upon them. And loving ourselves above all else we have not just been alienated from God, but alienated from each other. Every act of violence and cruelty is begotten from this one show of pomp, either through the evil that we do, or its consequences in the spoiling of other people's lives. And God will not stop us. We are only capable of love because we are equally capable of choosing not to love. But not stopping is not the same as not caring. God reaches out to show us how to live and how to love. The whole story of Jesus Christ is the story of a Father's love seeking out the wayward hearts of his beloved children. He breaks the heart that is wedded to self and offers to put a new heart within us if we are penitent.

We do therefore need to speak of sin. After all, Jesus begins his ministry with the words: 'Repent and believe the good news' (Mark 1:15). The good news is of the 'faithful love of God that extends from age to age' (Luke 1:40). The way we receive this good news is by repentance. This repentance is not just saying sorry, but a complete re-orientation of life. God becomes our centre, he takes his place on the throne of our heart. But there is a wonderful paradox. As we put God at the centre of our life, so he puts us at the centre of his. The words that Jesus said to Zacchaeus are said to us: 'I am going to stay at your house today' (Luke 19:6) Salvation comes to our lives. We therefore need to speak of what it means to be forgiven. In my experience more people have come to faith through the testimony of other Christians than through any other evangelistic strategy. And it is usually stories of being accepted and forgiven which most resonate with those who seek. I have also found that more Christians come to receive the grace of absolution in sacramental confession because other Christians have spoken about the difference it has made in their lives than because they have heard some exhortations from the pulpit. No wonder evangelism has been described as one beggar telling another beggar where to get bread!

Mary Recounts God's Justice

'Righteousness and justice are the foundations of his throne.' (Psalm 97:2)

> He has used the power of his arm,
> He has routed the arrogant of heart.
> He has pulled down princes from their thrones and
>   raised the lowly.
> He has filled the hungry with good things, sent the
>   rich away empty.

Mary sings of the kingdom that God is preparing, a kingdom of justice and mercy. In the end it is the combination of these two ideals that lifts the Christian vision above earthly utopias. Time and again human justice fails to be merciful, and human mercy ends up unjust. Even in the story of the prodigal son the Father succeeds in mercy towards his younger son, but fails in justice with the elder. The climax of the story is not the return of the prodigal, but the failure of the Father to reconcile the two sons.

The story pinpoints the painful quandaries of our lives and
directs us beyond ourselves to God. The psalmist recognizes that
only God can be merciful and just.

> 'Mercy and truth have met together;
> righteousness and peace have kissed each other.'
>
> (Psalm 85:11)

Thus Mary can pronounce with confidence the just and merciful
revolution of God; the upside down kingdom where the poor
and weak are exalted, the proud and arrogant put to rout.
Throughout Christian history the Church has failed again and
again to live out the radical vision of the Magnificat, preferring to
do business with the powerful than show solidarity with the
weak. But as we say the words of the Magnificat we cannot help
but shrink in recognition of the way the Church in the
prosperous West has reneged on the gospel. What irony that in
our own day we tear ourselves apart worrying over the legitimacy
of women priests, and now the rights and wrongs of homo-
sexuality, when the clear teaching of the gospel about money and
possession and status passes us by. Which is not to say there are
not legitimate questions concerning gender and sexuality, only
that we have quite comfortably allowed something so central to
the teaching of Jesus – the sombre warning of the corrupting
power of wealth and rank – to slip from the gospel story. Well,
we should let the words of Mary afflict us and disturb our comfort. The gospel story is of poverty receiving glory, of strength in
weakness. Mary not only tells this story, she embodies it through
her own surrender to God. Her song reminds the Church that
the proclamation of the gospel cannot be separated from the
building of the kingdom. Evangelism is not just about bringing
individuals to faith, it is about proclaiming justice.

> 'Mary, the first Christian Woman, is also the first revolution-
> ary of the new order. The Church, of which the Virgin is the
> type, cannot proclaim the good news of salvation without at
> the same time making the love of God concrete by the defence
> of justice for the poor and needy.[3]

Therefore when we engage in the ministry of evangelism not only should we boldly speak of the values of the Kingdom, we will find that it is often through our work to bring about this Kingdom that the best opportunities for evangelism will arise. When people see how much we care about the injustices of the world and the needs of the marginalized and poor, they will also see the efficacy of the gospel.

Mary Recalls God's Promise of Peace

'The Lord shall give his people the blessing of peace.' (Psalm 29:11)

> He has come to the help of Israel his servant, mindful of
>   his faithful love
> – according to the promise he made to our ancestors –
> of his mercy to Abraham and to his descendants for ever.

First of all, God shaped a nation to prepare the way for his coming. The Jewish people have always understood themselves to be God's chosen, a people called to reveal the holiness and righteousness of the one true God. Often in the Old Testament the people of Israel are personified as a woman, and sometimes the title 'Daughter of Zion' is used (Isaiah 62:11; Zephaniah 3:14; Zechariah 2:10). This concept is both mystical and eschatological. The Daughter of Zion is the one who embodies the union of Israel with her God, and the one who through her motherhood will bring deliverance of the Messianic hope. Luke clearly recognizes in the Virgin Mary the Daughter of Zion. She who conceives the Christ in her womb is full of grace, intimately united to God. And the Christ whom she bears is the Messiah, the one who will deliver his people and 'be a light of revelation to the gentiles' (Luke 2:32).

So, in the last few lines of the Magnificat, Mary announces that God's promises are being fulfilled. Because of his mercy and his faithful love, because he has not despised the lowliness of his hand-maiden, because he has heard the cry of his people, and because in Mary the creation says yes to God, peace is established, the work of reconciliation is begun.

The promise that was made to the ancestors of Israel is that God has come to reign. The angel says to Mary: 'The Lord God will give to Jesus the throne of his ancestor David; he will rule over the House of Jacob for ever and his reign will have no end' (Luke 1:32). Mary does not yet realize that God is also fulfilling the prophecy of Abraham, who foretold that 'God himself will provide the lamb for the sacrifice' (Genesis 22:8).

In this way we learn the true nature of Christian peace – not the silence after the guns have finished firing, but the painful embrace of reconciling love. Through the child growing in the womb of Mary, God is reconciling all things to himself, everything in heaven and everything on earth, and he will make peace through his death on the cross (see Colossians 1:20).

The Hebrew concept for this peace is 'shalom'. It describes wholeness and completeness, an integrity and a harmony that brings to fulfilment all the many strands of God's creation. God used Mary to bring this shalom to the world because of her co-operation with his will. Today he asks us if we will co-operate with his will and bear Jesus to the world. And though we may shrink from the enormity of this task, the hard truth about being a Christian is that we really have no choice. Each one of us is called to be a witness to Jesus. Whether we like it or not, our lives bear testimony to the gospel. Once people know that we are Christian, or even that we attend Church, they will make judgements about the efficacy and veracity of the gospel on the evidence of our lives. Once we have said yes to God, we are witnesses to Christ.

Mary shows us how we can be faithful witnesses. Most of all, she models for us strong Christian living. Evangelism is about making Jesus known. Mary can help us because she always points the way to Jesus. 'Do whatever he tells you' (John 2:6), she says to the servants at the wedding at Cana. Behold Jesus, she proclaims in silent witness from her vigil at the Cross. Just as the Holy Spirit came upon her to form Jesus in her womb, so the Holy Spirit can come upon us to form Jesus in our lives. The promise of peace and wholeness that was made to Abraham is made to us.

One final thing. Sometimes evangelism is seen as either the shallow end of faith – the preserve of the mindlessly enthusiastic – or the macho branch of the Church – tub-thumping proclamation and feverish activity. Mary presents another way. Through her Magnificat we see the proclamation of salvation properly bound up with the proclamation of the Kingdom. By her example we learn a contemplative approach to evangelism. She is never afraid to witness to her son, and never afraid to face the suffering that this witness brings, but she is not a preacher, nor a strategist, nor a leader. She is simply the one who, filled with grace and joy, treasures the marvellous works of God in her heart (Luke 2:52), and is therefore able to live a life translucent of the gospel. What was true for Mary can be true for us. We can be Christ's witnesses today. Nothing is impossible to God.

Notes

1. Elizabeth Jennings, 'The Visitation', from *Collected Poems*, Carcanet Press, 1986, pp. 46–7.
2. Gerard Manley Hopkins, 'God's Grandeur', from *Poems and Prose*, Penguin Books, 1953, p. 27.
3. Max Thurian, *Mary, Mother of the Lord, Figure of the Church*, Mowbray, 1963, p. 93.

Sacred Spaces in Secular Culture.

Madeleine Bunting

When I was asked to give a paper on 'Sacred Spaces in Secular Culture' by Walsingham for their Conference in Oxford, I immediately made a mistake. Unhesitatingly, I interpreted the brief as metaphor, I didn't think of physical places, but the values and ideas held holy by the unchurched.

When I discovered the rest of the programme was devoted to such subjects as the cathedral, and when it belatedly dawned on me that Walsingham had a particular interest in sacred space, the mistake itself became telling. Reflecting on it, I concluded there is no collectively recognized sacred space in secular culture in terms of a physical place (unless you count an art exhibition, with its reverential crowds).

Every major faith has always had at the heart of its practice a building, in which people collect for ritual; the temple, the church, the synagogue, the mosque or the gurdwara. The distinctive characteristic of the secular West is the decline in this sort of religious activity. For generations, enormous economic, artistic, emotional and communal resources were invested in constructing and using a shared sacred space. No longer.

This reveals two aspects of contemporary spirituality. First, its fragmentation: people may still have physical places which they invest with sacred significance, but it is a private, highly personal attachment. It is not shared and commonly recognized as sacred. It could be a particular tor on Dartmoor, a mountain in Scotland, a street in Manchester where they were born, a beach in Devon of childhood summers, or a London park. (It could even be a cathedral – although the sacred significance attached to it is not of the birth, death and resurrection of the Son of God, but a response to the beauty and age of the building.)

Secondly, a lot of people would not ascribe any physical place as a sacred space. Yes, cathedrals, lakes, beaches are beautiful, but 'sacred' is a very, very serious word. Sacred is that which is most precious, most integral to our understanding of life; to many people now that is something they place within themselves, not in a particular place. They have internalized sacred space.

Our relationship to place has been transformed in the course of the 20th century. Most of us are no longer living where we were born; most of us will move several times to completely different areas of the country – even perhaps the world – in the course of our lives. Even more importantly, speed of movement is now built into the fabric of our lives. People commute hundreds of miles in a day, and travel thousands of miles in the space of a few hours for a two-week holiday. E.M. Forster's *Howard's End* prophetically identified the threat posed by the motor car to an intimate, intense relationship with place.

Another development also explains this privatization of sacred space: urbanization. The vast majority of us now live in cities. There has been fascinating research (by Comedia) tracing how the public life of the street has been undermined by traffic, crime and the fear of crime. We have retreated, physically and emotionally, behind our front door into our nuclear families – fearful of mugging and children being knocked down by speeding cars, alienated by dog dirt, car fumes and intrusive advertising. Behind that front door, we want the home and garden to become a refuge – in many cases a sacred refuge, given the elaborate care lavished upon it – from the competitive, insecure world of work and city. This overloading of our home and immediate family with a heavy burden of expectation has generated problems we know only too well. The massive growth and fascination in interior decor, DIY and gardening, with the proliferation of magazines and television programmes devoted to the subject, is evidence of this homage to household gods.

But ultimately, just as Jews under threat of persecution historically developed skills and trading assets which were ultimately transportable, such as banking and diamonds, so in our secular, urban culture, people internalize sacred space. They have made themselves transportable. When someone is mugged in your neighbourhood, you can continue to live there, such is your detachment from your immediate physical environment.

This internalized, individualized sacred space is what erupted spectacularly into public life at Princess Diana's death. in August 1997. Reams has been written on the individual, highly personal nature of the momentoes which accumulated in the Mall and at the gates of Kensington Palace. Reams has been written on how the Princess had come to mean something very intimate to millions of strangers. Ever since her death, Christians have been pondering, rather like the Spanish *conquistadors* hankered after their Latin American gold, how they could tap into this vast subterranean pool of vibrant, passionate spirituality. There was the unfortunate report on the BBC news when the Archbishop of Canterbury fumbled for words to articulate his understanding of this 'inchoate' spirituality and urged churchgoers to speak more clearly and directly to it. Later, posters went up with the image of the heaps of flowers offered at Diana's death, urging people to church at Easter.

There are two things which I find, as a Christian, acutely embarrassing about this desperate desire to turn Diana's death into an opportunity for evangelism. First, Christians are showing about as much sensitivity as the *conquistadors*. In the rush to replace Diana with Jesus, there was precious little attempt to understand the nature of the sacred space people revealed in their lives in that extraordinary week. Immediately it was being over-laid with what it really meant according to a Christian template – for example, sanctification, the search for a madonna – or what it could come to mean, given the right (i.e. Christian) kind of guidance.

Secondly, the triumphant way in which Christians seized upon this event as proof (a) that people still believed in God, (b) that people still needed to go to church and (c) that Christianity was still relevant. All of these were half true, but the conclusion – that there was a crop of good souls out there just waiting to be harvested – was most certainly not. That people use the Church when they see fit, and still believe in God, is not evidence that they are about to become fervent Christians. People use Church as they also use astrology, Feng-shui and yoga.

The gulf between the churched and the unchurched was even more painfully demonstrated in the idea of linking Diana and Easter for the churches' advertising campaign. Only a Christian could possibly explain the connection: Diana's death, and life after death granted after the resurrection of Jesus Christ. In September 1997, people went to the church and they said the Our Father in Hyde Park, but does that mean they believe in life after death or the resurrection? No.

The first characteristic – and most obvious departure from traditional Christianity – of privatized sacred space is that it does not represent, nor search for, absolute truth. At the risk of dangerously stereotyping a phenomenon which is deeply individual, privatized sacred space is not abstract and it is not cosmic, it recognizes no external authority. It is focused on the self.

The sacred narrative has moved from the cosmic – the Creation, Fall and Redemption by God's only Son – to telling the story of the individual's journey through life. We each develop a narrative, heavily influenced by psychotherapeutic concepts, in which we explain and seek to understand the twists and turns of our lives. Self-knowledge has replaced knowledge of God as the ultimate objective.

In this sacred space, the greatest virtue is being true to oneself; that is the final arbiter of moral decisions. Other virtues include honesty, emotional courage and tolerance of the decisions others make on their life journey. What simply doesn't exist in this sacred space are some of the virtues most highly praised in traditional Christianity, such as duty, obligation, responsibility and self-sacrifice.

The paradox about the highly personal, sacred narrative we are engaged in constructing is our compulsion to tell everyone else about it. Everywhere in the media, you see people baring their souls – the phrase is absolutely accurate. Newspapers are saturated with interviews in which celebrities (or nonentities) will tell their innermost secrets, and our fascination in other people's stories is seemingly inexhaustible. Even as we deny our collective nature, we still desperately need to relate our experience of the sacred with that of other people.

Madonna, the pop icon, has always had an uncanny ability to interpret and formulate the mood of the times. She has also always been fascinated by religious imagery and language, and never more so than with the release of her album, *Ray of Light*. In an interview in *New Musical Express*, she described how she had grown disenchanted with her immense wealth:

> I am just beginning to have the things I really need and beginning to have things that are really important, which is intimacy and love and children ... The other things exhibitionism, all of those things are not nothing, they're ... fantastic expressions, manifestations of loneliness, or despair or curiosity, but ultimately they never take the place of the really important things. So when you have a lot of that other stuff, fame, fortune, celebrity, whatever, and you get tons and tons, and tons of it and you realise that ultimately that it isn't going to make you happy then you do say, 'Well, hold on then, there's got to be something more to this.'

She went on to explain where her search had taken her; interestingly, she had picked up bits and pieces of traditional religions. She studies the Jewish mystical tradition of kabbala, has private tutorings in Hinduism, and spends two hours a day in yoga. But there's not much evidence of the morality of traditional religion in her life decisions. She defends her choice to have her baby, Lourdes, without a stable relationship with the father: 'It's sad, it's not a perfect, ideal situation. It's much better for a family to be whole, but y'know, you have to be true to yourself and you have to be happy and if a situation is better one way than the other then that's the way to go.'

In another recent newspaper article on mothers who leave their children, the theme of being true to self reappeared. One interviewee, Morgan, returned her children to her husband after six years without any warning. It was explained thus:

> The 'heart-wrenching' decision was prompted by the realisation that she had to do more with her life and only had a limited amount of time in which to act. 'I felt trapped. I was living on income support. I had no dignity, and I knew I had to work to get back my self-respect. If I'd waited until the children were grown up, it would have been too late. It seemed

to me that my ex-husband had had all these years of freedom and that it was my turn.'

It's not hard to see why Princess Diana echoed the sacred space of millions of women. She was perceived to be trying to be true to herself within an institution dedicated to a stifling concept of duty; she was perceived as emotionally honest about her faults and weaknesses; she was perceived as having the courage to search for love – to the point of adultery – and to refuse to accept a soul-destroying, loveless marriage.

There is another dimension to our privatized sacred space. As we have lost a geographical sense of roots, and of belonging, we have turned towards our family to compensate and to provide a sense of our origins. Margaret Forster's moving book *Hidden Lives*, about three generations of her family, comments at the end, 'We are our past, especially our family past, a truism if ever there was one.'

There has been a publishing boom in confessional family memoirs, such as Blake Morrison's *And When Did You Last See Your Father?* and Germaine Greer's *Daddy, We Hardly Knew You.* The journalist Angela Neustatter, commenting on the phenomenon, writes,

> It is a kind of literary lifting of the crazy-paving that has covered daily existence in order to make sense of chimera relationships, intimate bonds distorted in a way that has not made sense, an unknown heritage

Neustatter herself links the trend for family memoirs with the decline in conventional religion; suggesting that it offers a substitute support system for religion in an age of 'mass atheism'.

The publishing boom is the visible tip of a widespread trend. There are an estimated 110,000 therapists in this country – compared to 11,000 Anglican priests and 6,000 Catholic priests. If each therapist is seeing 10 patients (a conservative estimate), then more than a million people are in therapy at any one time. Thousands more read self-help books loosely based on psychotherapeutic techniques, hundreds of which are produced every year. We are all excavating our emotional past, trying to find resolution and reconciliation in old conflicts.

We are all to some extent influenced by a culture saturated by concepts drawn from psychotherapy, psychoanalysis and psychology. As Jenny Diski, author of *Skating to Antarctica*, an attempt to come to terms with her estranged mother, admits 'I am not immune to the power of popular psychology, for all my doubts and irritations with it.'

Again, the astonishing paradox is evident that while this search for origins, for understanding of how the past made you, is highly personal and individual, there is a compulsion to tell others about it. Some tell their therapist, and the analogies with the confessional box are obvious. Some tell the world by publishing deeply personal, excruciatingly honest accounts. Linda Grant, who wrote *Tell Me Who I Am Again*, admits the book explained why she and her sister put their mother with Alzheimer's disease in a home:

> I don't think the book resolved anything with my mother, but I do see the book as a public explanation of who I am, and yes, it matters to me that people who know my writing understand why I am the way I am.

Sacred space in secular culture serves the same purpose as all sacred space – to answer the questions 'Who am I?', 'Where do I come from?' and 'What is the meaning of life?' At some points, and I have quoted a few above, it comes into direct conflict with any traditional religious understanding of the sacred: how could a mother turn her back on the most sacred bond of all? How could a mother deny her child a father? At other points, the two approaches are not so far apart; both share a strong emphasis for reconciliation. In a religious context, that reconciliation is with God; in a secular context, that reconciliation of acceptance and forgiveness is primarily with oneself – a task not to be underestimated in our competitive culture steeped in images of perfection and high performance. To a lesser extent, it is reconciliation with others; interestingly, the bulk of family memoirs take as their starting point a difficult relationship with a parent.

This sacred space, for all its faults, humanizes our culture. At its best, it values humility and emotional generosity. What worries me is that, within a couple of decades, it might come to be seen as outdated romanticism of the 20th century. There are two threats looming; first, the huge advances in genetic science and knowledge of the brain look set to challenge our beliefs about who we are and the nature of personality. The second threat is already widely evident in our culture. It is the nightmare scenario conjured up in *The Culture of Narcissism* and *The Minimal Self* by C. Lasch. A society predicated on change and performance where we reduce our self to a residual minimum for psychic survival. As David Kennard and Neil Small summed it up in *Living Together*, a collection of essays by psychoanalysts and psychotherapists:

> We thought we had limitless options without consequences, the freedom to choose everything at once. It was a form of narcissism in which we defined who we were through our purchases and our opinion polls, our opinions shaped by the communication industry. We became commodities ourselves, living in a world where reality and fantasy converged and where our stance was to adjust, to survive. Looking backwards generates a debilitating nostalgia and forwards engenders a dread of the future and a concern with preparing defences against it.

PART IV

Revealed in Art

Mary's Discipleship and the Artistic Imagination

David Brown

Walk into the Walker Gallery in Liverpool, and there you will encounter an early 14th-century painting by Simone Martini of events subsequent to the 12-year old Jesus being lost in the Temple. Mary and Joseph have at last found him, and Joseph, the central figure, is querying the boy's actions by pointing accusingly at Mary, who sits exhausted on the left and also holds out a pleading hand to her son on the right. The most interesting feature of the painting, though, is Jesus' response. He stands with his arms crossed, and with a face like any other little boy in a huff or sulk, who has just taken umbrage at his parents' reprimand. One can almost hear him silently saying, 'how dare you speak to me like that,' and no doubt many of us will at that point recall similar actions and responses from our own childhood. Now cross the Channel to Cologne, and there you will find a 20th-century work by Max Ernst, the German title of which translates as 'Mary spanks the infant Jesus in front of three witnesses'. That is indeed what is happening, with Jesus over Mary's knee and her hand raised to strike, while three bystanders look on. When first shown in 1923 it produced much controversy, and indeed so shocked were some of the Christians of Cologne that it had to be withdrawn from exhibition and kept in storage for several years.

Two paintings, six centuries apart, but both may be used to introduce the issue which I wish to address in this essay: the extent to which the relevance of Mary to our lives can be distorted by a suffocating piety that excludes her from some of the most characteristic features of our own humanity. Below I shall focus on paintings where Mary's role is more central, but I have begun with these two because they illustrate the way in which similar issues are raised by how we tell the story of Jesus as well. The advantage of beginning there is because, if even in case of Christ (where divinity and humanity are embodied in one person) the human dimension has to be taken with more seriousness, then so much more so will this be true of Mary who remains solely human, however powerfully graced she may have been.

Consider then these two specific cases, sulking and punishment. In an earlier age Christians might well have been inclined to deny that either could ever have been true of Jesus' growth to adulthood. They would have been seen as undermining any claim to his perfection. But contemporary child psychology suggests a different answer. We are now acutely aware of the extent to which the identity of a child is forged by testing boundaries. Searching for a defined security, it spends much of its time exploring limits and, somewhat paradoxically, finds its reassurance in the parental 'No'. Nowadays, this is less commonly given through corporal punishment, but matters were quite otherwise in the first century. So it would seem that reflections on the customs of the time and on child psychology alike, force us in the same direction, towards the recognition that these two artists offer us better insight into the early life of Jesus than more pietistic sentiment. It is also important to note that what we might describe in the actions of an adult as unqualifiedly wrong, does not necessarily admit of the same description for a child. Children are, after all, still learning.

Whether or not my two examples carry conviction with the reader, some reassurance may be found in the fact that it is in some ways a less severe version of the same problem that I want to address here in respect of Mary. Childhood is all about growth and development, but so too normally is discipleship. So one question that arises is the extent to which it might be legitimate to apply such language of growth to Mary. Certainly, if so, it would bring one great advantage, in a deeper sense of the way in which Mary can help us in our own discipleship. Where my argument will end is with the contention that, if we take such an approach as our starting point, the Assumption becomes its natural conclusion. But I must begin elsewhere, and indeed with an objection: that it is inappropriate to characterize Mary as a disciple at all. Not only was she not one of the twelve, but also even in that wider sense in which all of us are disciples, there is something wrong in so characterizing her since, unlike us, she was vouchsafed a unique knowledge of her son's role and a special intimacy in its fulfilment.

Yet, without denying that unique role, against such an objection must be set the way in which modern biblical scholarship has transformed our understanding of the life of Jesus and thus, by implication, that of Mary also. Jesus' consciousness of his mission appears to have developed gradually, as did the significance attached to that mission by his immediate followers. The trinitarian formula with which Matthew's Gospel ends, for example, has no parallel in the rest of the narrative.[1] Our four gospels were, in fact, all written in the light of the confidence that the resurrection had brought, and so things are inevitably presented as running much more smoothly than they are likely to have been experienced at the time. It is hardly surprising, therefore, that reading between the lines we sometimes discover quite a different picture. It is, I suggest, in that light that we should consider those passages that might be taken to imply opposition to Jesus from his own family during the course of his ministry.[2] In the subsequent history of the Church alternative explanations have often been sought, but is it not more natural to read them at their face value? James 'the Lord's brother', for instance, does not appear to have become a disciple until after the crucifixion.[3] Might the encounters, therefore, not be more naturally taken to suggest a family puzzled by Jesus' behaviour, worried by the direction his life was taking, and concerned to mitigate any possible threat to his own safety that this implied.[4] Thus, for the best of motives, they try to intervene, and only later comprehend why his mission had to take the form it did.

Mary is by implication sometimes included in such family opposition.[5] This might, though, seem incompatible with Luke's infancy narrative, but is it? For, no matter how literally we take his account, the events in question would surely not have brought quite the certainty that we now retrospectively and instinctively feel they must have had. For Mary to have been told that her child would have a very special role is hardly the same thing as recognizing his identity as God incarnate, nor indeed would the right categories have been in place at the time for Mary to comprehend any such claim. All that was to come later. Again, even a virgin birth would not have seemed quite so astounding as it seems to us today, as the repeated rumours of such occurrences through history indicate. Nor were the facts of biology fully known, and so, though strange, a virgin birth would not have seemed quite so unique as to mean only one thing.[6] Because artists have had as part of their aim not only the wish to satisfy their clerical patrons but also the desire to engage the viewer's imagination, they have sometimes been better than theologians at reflecting on such issues. For engaging the viewer requires some sense of identification on our part with Mary, and that has usually involved stressing the more human side of her story. What, therefore, I suggest we do is examine how artistic representations of her life have reflected such questions, and then attempt to draw some conclusions. So far as possible, I shall confine my examples to illustrations drawn from the kind of gallery art with which the reader is likely already to have had some direct acquaintance.

Let us begin then with the Annunciation. One debate that is very obvious in paintings on the theme is the question of how Mary and the angel should regard one another. Should Mary kneel before Gabriel, overwhelmed as well she might be by the stupendous task which she has been assigned, or should Gabriel kneel before her as a sign of the respect due to her, either because of her own inherent qualities for the role or else because of the honour due to the child she will eventually bear. In the National Gallery in London there is a couple of paintings from the late 15th century that make the angel kneel, while in the frescoes he painted for the Arena Chapel at Padua, Giotto, early in the previous century, solved the problem by making both appear to kneel.[7] But might not Mary alone kneeling better capture her humanity and innocence? It suggests that she is still learning her role. That Giotto's contemporary, Duccio, has both figures standing indicates how open options still remained at this time.[8] All, though, follow Luke, and indicate some degree of trepidation, most commonly through Mary holding her hand against her breast.[9] But that is quite a minor gesture compared to Dante Gabriel Rossetti's cowering figure of 1850, now in the Tate.[10] Mary is curled up on her bed against the wall as the angel addresses her, holding a lily. The strength of the painting is the way in which the starkness of the scene helps us to feel ourselves alongside Mary as she (and we) wrestle with God's purpose for our lives. For a more contemporary example one might turn to Durham Cathedral, and its recently installed sculpture by the Polish artist, Josef Pyrz.[11] While the concave belly successfully represents receptivity, the prominence of the veins on the young girl's neck underlines all the tensions involved in seeking to understand, and yield to, the divine will. Touching the wooden neck, one becomes acutely aware of the alarm that must have been felt by Mary in facing a future which she only imperfectly understood.[12]

None of this is intended to imply the complete failure of other ways of representing the event, but it is to question how such paintings are most appropriately read in terms of continuing religious relevance. Take an extreme instance from the National Gallery: Crivelli's *Annunciation*. Mary is here portrayed as a woman of considerable wealth who kneels, reading at her *prie-dieu*, as Gabriel also kneels. Although the fashionable emphasis in our own day on the poverty of the Holy Family may well be exaggerated, a painting like this that goes to the other extreme is even more implausible. If then it is read in any sense as the assertion of fact, one can only come away disappointed. But an alternative approach is available. Painted as it was to celebrate the granting of limited self-government to the small town of Ascoli Piceno in the Italian Marches, it can be read as an attempt to imply the continuing relevance of the annunciation to the lives of the painter's clients. God brought joy once to Mary through the sending of the Holy Spirit, but this has now happened for them in their own small way. For in the distance the carrier pigeon that brought the news of the town's new status is seen. To us today it may seem disrespectful to compare the work of the Holy Spirit with a mere pigeon, but undoubtedly the intention is to assert the continuing activity of God in people's lives.

When one turns to Nativity scenes, one is immediately confronted by the present trend within the Church to decry the type of art we find in galleries and from which my examples have hitherto been drawn, with preference almost automatically given to the more austere iconography of the Byzantine tradition, which is seen as more spiritual. One wonders, though, whether much of this critique is not in fact based on misunderstanding, as though sentimentality were the sole, or even the primary, reason for Renaissance painting. We have lost the capacity to experience the more allusive style of symbolism in such depictions, and so our capacity to respond to the paintings at an appropriate level. To take a specific example, like early medieval art Byzantine often anticipates the crucifixion explicitly by having the crib in the shape of a flat altar,[13] but the same symbolism is also there in Renaissance painting, though more indirectly. Thus the presence of a goldfinch in paintings by Raphael and others indicates not a pleasant toy for the child, but his future crown of thorns, since that particular bird was then well known to feed on thistle thorns. To my mind it is unlikely that Mary had at this stage quite so specific a knowledge about what would happen to her son, but the symbolism can still speak of her envisaging a mission for her son which is troubling precisely because it is so uncertain. The sadness of so many a Renaissance Madonna and Child thus continues to have point.

Thanks to the influence of works like Pseudo-Bonaventure's *Meditations* medieval Christians were encouraged to envisage themselves as themselves present at such scenes, and even as participants.[14] In earlier iconography one of the two midwives is depicted washing the child, but as Mary came to be seen as herself a suitable medium for relating us to the child, she was duly assigned this role as well. A particularly fine example in the National Gallery comes from the 15th-century Flemish painter, Robert Campin. Once more Mary is portrayed as part of a wealthy home, but counterpoised to this is the presence in front of the fireplace of a small basin ready for her, herself to bathe the infant Jesus. The necessity of service to Christ, and thereby to others, is thus indicated through Mary, wealthy woman though she is, nonetheless taking on the role of a servant. The imaginative exercise of oneself helping to bathe Jesus may not be something that comes naturally to the modern mind, but once again it adds a learning dimension to discipleship for both Mary and ourselves. Although it is not impossible that the Holy Family had servants,[15] what is more important to note here is the way in which Mary is given the role of initiating us into tasks of service with which neither she nor the viewer, it is assumed, will be familiar.

My earlier discussion of Martini's painting has already offered one example of how Jesus' growth to adulthood might be treated. For another consider John Everett Millais' painting in the Tate of *Christ in the House of his Parents*, again from 1850. In the midst of a rather dirty and untidy carpenter's workshop Jesus is portrayed centre-stage, with his mother anxiously kneeling before him as she examines his hand bleeding from a nail used in the door Joseph is making. The symbolism of the future piercing on the cross is obvious, but it was in fact a painting that aroused considerable opposition at the time, including from Charles Dickens and *The Times*' art critic. Its source, though, was not the symbolism, but what was seen as excessive realism in the depiction of the infant's world: 'the attempt to associate the holy family with the meanest details of a carpenter's shop, with no conceivable omission of misery, of dirt, of even disease ... is disgusting'.[16] But against such criticism must be set the sense of Jesus' full involvement in the ordinary human condition. Dickens describes Mary as 'so horrible in her ugliness that ... she would stand out from the rest of the company as a monster in the vilest cabaret in France or in the lowest gin-shop in England'.[17] It is the gross exaggeration and caricature that one has come to expect of polemic, but from it we may draw a serious point. In contrast to her child, whose face remains untroubled, Mary looks anxious and pre-occupied, and that in part explains the reason for the 'dislocated neck', of which Dickens also complains. Her gaze is torn between the child's injured hand and his calm face, and this is reflected in her own ruffled brow. What that brow surely indicates is her anxious realization that the responsibility for her son's mission, however little she understands it, still at this stage lies primarily with her.

Eventually, though, Jesus' unclouded childhood had to yield to the necessity of him acting in his own right. Cana is the first incident where a new kind of relationship with his mother is implied. The way in which Mary takes the initiative provides a useful counter to those who claim that the image of Mary has only ever reinforced the passivity of women. Even so, there is a certain sharpness to the exchange that could be taken to indicate a new kind of relationship emerging between them. For, although Jesus accedes to Mary's request, he makes it clear that it is now up to him to determine when 'his hour has come'.[18] We are all aware of adults whose psychological growth has been thwarted by their parents' refusal to allow them sufficient space to forge their own distinctive adult identity. That happens because parents never find it easy to accept all the elements of difference that now begin to arise between parent and child. Have we any reason to think the story of the incarnation proceeded otherwise? Indeed, might the assertion of difference have proved much more traumatic in this case, precisely because of Jesus' perception that his mission involved a testing call to suffering and not unalloyed triumph? The nature of the exchange at Cana might then be seen as reflecting the wider pattern of family conflict that we noted earlier. Mary had, like us, to struggle towards full acceptance of Jesus' mission as he understood it and not as she naturally wished it as a mother.

Among biblical scholars the incident at Cana is often thought not to be historical but, rather, symbolic of the new life and power that the gospel brings, and in favour of such a view is the various symbolic elements in the narrative, among them the absurd over-provision of wine: 120 gallons.[19] This is not the place to enter into such debates, except to observe that, as we shall note later with some other incidents, the more important issue is not its actual occurrence or otherwise but whether it is the sort of thing that might have happened, in the sense of whether it fits well or not with what we already know to be true of Jesus and Mary. In other words, the point is that fact is not the only way to understand; imaginative insight can also help. Sadly, though, this is one instance where I have been unable to find a painting that significantly advances our understanding of Mary as disciple. The most famous, that by Paolo Veronese and now in the Louvre, is almost wholly secular in feel, overwhelmed as the miracle is by its architectural setting, but even someone like Giotto, who gives Mary a central place in issuing the command, offers us none of the complicated dynamic that we find in John's Gospel, and in fact in most versions the incident is usurped for its potential eucharistic symbolism, something that is already happening even in its earliest occurrence on the 5th-century wooden door of St Sabina at Rome.

A better example for the value of imaginative insight might therefore be an incident which does not occur in the gospels at all, but became frequent in painting: Christ taking leave of his Mother. It was felt certain that Jesus must have shared with his mother his decision to go to the cross before the final, fateful events began to unfold. In a painting in the National Gallery in Edinburgh, Benozzo Gozzoli places the incident at the beginning of the road to Calvary, but the more normal pattern is to be found in Albrecht Altdorfer's better known painting in London. Set in the countryside, Mary swoons against the backdrop of a decaying building, while to the right the figures of Christ and St John are unnaturally elongated, to suggest their growth into the light, an implication further accentuated by the tall trees behind them. It is an uncomfortable image that reminds us of Jesus' words that 'there has arisen no one greater than John the Baptist, yet he who is least in the kingdom of heaven is greater than he'.[20] In other words, like the Baptist Mary has to come to terms here with her life hitherto as part of an order that is vanishing and which must now give place to something better. As such there are, of course, lessons for our own discipleship, as we struggle to interpret our past in ways that value its integrity but are, at the same time, compatible with God's call for us to enter new and different patterns.

Such a contrast between past and present is also how some biblical commentators interpret John's intention in placing Mary and the Beloved Disciple at the foot of the cross. She is there, it is suggested, to represent the old order of Israel being entrusted to the care of the new Church, represented by John, or else, put more positively, Lady Zion giving birth to a new community.[21] Certainly, there are considerable difficulties in the way of regarding the incident as purely historical, if only because the other three evangelists declare that Jesus' disciples 'all forsook him, and fled', while the women witnesses to the crucifixion (among whom Mary is not mentioned) are placed at some distance, 'looking on from afar'.[22] Moreover, it is hard to think of either the Roman authorities, or even Jesus himself, as encouraging such close proximity. To the former she would have appeared as simply a nuisance, while would not her son have himself sought to lessen her pain by discouraging her immediate presence?

But, whatever the historical truth, imaginatively it is entirely right that Mary should be there and with her us also as we seek to follow her in her discipleship. Perhaps as a matter of fact she underwent a more private agony, cared for by some of the apostles or other women at home, but what we know of her later life indicates clearly enough that, in due course, she did come to a fuller realization of the significance of her son's death. In conveying that significance, it is fascinating to observe the hesitancy of both artists and their clients over the extent to which it was appropriate for Mary to mediate such contemplation. Fra Angelico's *Crucifixion*, for instance, is replete with symbolism to guide us: Adam's skull lies at the base of the cross on which the new Adam hangs, while the cross itself at its top turns into a tree of life in which a pelican is perched, ready to feed its young with its own blood.[23] But it is John who sheds the tears rather than Mary, and in fact various Counter- Reformation treatises recommended that Mary must not be shown to swoon.[24] Among the reasons for the restriction were the conviction that not only did Mary have no sins of her own for which to weep, she also must have known the eventual outcome and so this indicated restraint. But neither factor seems to me compelling. As our Lord's own cry of dereliction indicates, matters did not proceed quite so smoothly, while even if Mary had no sins of her own, there was still a world out there that made the crucifixion inevitable. Artistic representation of the extremes of emotion can thus still have their point in enabling us to lament with Mary over our own sins. From the 19th century Delacroix offers us a particularly powerful example of such an approach,[25] while an alternative image that, in the 16th century came to be regarded as more acceptable but also allows such mediation, was the Pietà. Such an image first became common in 14th-century Germany, and was still relatively unfamiliar in Italy when Michelangelo sculpted his famous example at the beginning of the 16th century. But it soon became normative in mediating such reflection.

At least as early as Ambrose, the inference was also being

drawn that Mary must have been granted an appearance of her resurrected son.[26] However, there are surprisingly few artistic representations, Dürer's being perhaps among the better known.[27] Their relative infrequency, though, does not betoken any hostility to the notion, but rather its relative redundancy in comparison with another incident which could more powerfully express Mary's final position in discipleship. For in the opening chapter of Acts Luke records Mary's presence among the incipient Church, and it seemed, therefore, not an unreasonable inference to draw from this that she must also have been present at Pentecost, recorded in the following chapter. What is fascinating about the history of the iconography of this scene is the way in which the inference eventually led to Mary commonly being given central place.

Although this pattern occurs as early as the 6th century, and is common from the 12th, artists and patrons appear to have continued to debate its legitimacy, in part because of the questions it raised about leadership and ordination. Two paintings from around 1500 may be used to illustrate the issue of appropriate limits. Although both have Mary in the centre, Martin Schongauer's version is relatively restrained, while Juan de Flanders makes a seated and reading Mary quite dominate the scene.[28] Occasionally, it is possible to demonstrate that female painter took particular delight in its representation. One such example would be the 17th-century Portuguese artist, Josefa d'Óbidos. But perhaps more pertinent for feminist concerns is the more widely disseminated practice of Mary being depicted reading. Originally intended in paintings of the Annunciation to allude to Isaiah's prophecy,[29] the practice quickly came to function as an argument for the entitlement of women to education. So, when combined as here with Mary being given a leadership role, it helps undermine any exaggerated claims about portrayals of Mary having always worked in the past to the detriment of women, in encouraging subordination and passivity.

Even so, from the 17th century onwards it is a version of Pentecost that became less frequent. A conspicuous exception, though, comes from El Greco. Now in the Prado in Madrid, tongues of flame descend from a dove with wings outstretched, light from which forms an oval shape enveloping the assembled company. It is almost as though El Greco wishes to suggest that the Spirit has laid a vast egg, the yoke at the heart of which is Mary. Put in more modern terms, one might say that her long struggle to comprehend her son and his mission has at last reached fruition. There she is at the centre of the new community that he has founded. Some may wish to resist any such notion of growth in understanding on Mary's part, as though this must inevitably detract from her status. The alternative is to consider whether it might not actually enhance her significance for us. Certainly in our own pilgrimage of faith it is a matter of working gradually through the implications of Christ's life for our own, and, if Mary can do this alongside us, she will be there in the narrative as fellow traveller and not merely as someone essentially beyond our own struggles.

But it is not only in the narrative that she will be present, for we have not as yet reached the end of the story. Mary, like all other human beings, finally died. If we suppose her knowledge complete from the beginning, then her subsequent exaltation to heaven can read only as the endorsement of what she has been all along, and so of less relevance to us, who are essentially still on a path of pilgrimage. But if we allow development, then a different story can be told, not of course of her achieving anything by her own efforts but of her, through God's grace, being raised to a new status as disciple as well as mother that then makes her further exaltation to heaven doubly appropriate. Perhaps the difference I am trying to highlight can be most effectively indicated by contrasting two paintings of the Assumption, one by El Greco and the other by Rubens. Given the current reputation of these two masters, most readers will probably instantly assume that it is El Greco that I am about to go on to praise, but it seems to me that on this occasion at least it is Rubens who did the better job.[30] Once again, El Greco employs his oval shape in an attempt to bond heaven and earth, but the absence of movement between the two spheres and the sharpness of the line dividing them means that in the end one's final impression is of a division that remains as firm as ever. In one clear sense Mary has gone where she belongs and that is why we belong elsewhere, firmly here on earth. By contrast, Rubens' painting is full of movement and does much to hint at the apostles also being drawn by her to heaven. For, although she travels so fast to heaven that the angels have scarcely time to put on her crown, the bodies of the apostles all veer in the same direction, upwards and to the right. Therein lies a marked contrast to El Greco's painting where some of the disciples even face away, among them the one to whom El Greco has given his own face. Their averted gaze may add to the dignity of Mary's exalted state, but it is Rubens who tells us that the place where she has gone can also be ours. She has become the disciple who leads us to our ultimate destiny.

In presenting the Assumption in this way I do not mean to imply that this is the only argument that can be given in its favour.[31] Far from it! But it is all that needs to be said here to indicate that interpreting Mary's life in terms of discipleship need not necessarily have any deleterious consequences for Catholic doctrine. That said, the more important question remains: whether, as the modern Church continues to find fresh significance in the humanity of Christ, it is not high time for a similar approach to be applied to Mary? That way, her discipleship can become truly the pattern for our own.

Notes

1. Matt. 28:19; significantly, words of the resurrected Christ.
2. Mark 3:31–5; 6:1–6; Luke 8:19–21; 11:27–8; John 7:5.
3. His prominence in Acts must have come in part as a result of his resurrection appearance: I Cor. 15:7.
4. Added probability is given to this supposition if Mark 3:31–5 is read in conjunction with Mark 3:19–21.
5. At least in Mark.
6. The ovum was only discovered in 1827, while belief in supernaturally caused pregnancies and in parthenogenesis continued until modern times. For the former, think of the medieval incubus; for the latter the beliefs of Trobriand islanders and Australian Aborigines.
7. Both figures are made the same height, but interpretation is complicated by the fact that Mary has one leg raised. Was she about to kneel, but stopped by the angel? Fra Filippo Lippi's version in the National Gallery shares a similar ambiguity in that, though the angel alone kneels, Mary is seated in a humble position, whereas the version by the anonymous Master of Liesborn leaves us in no doubt about the inferiority of the angel: not only does he alone kneel, he is also dwarfed by a seated Mary.

8. The relevant portion of Duccio's *Maestà* is in the National Gallery, the rest in the cathedral museum in Siena.

9. Luke 1:29: 'she was greatly troubled at the saying' (RSV).

10. Actually painted in 1849, but given the date March 1850 on the canvass to provide an additional allusion to the Annunciation.

11. A wooden statue placed in the centre of Durham's Lady chapel, the Galilee.

12. For another modern example, see J. McEwen, *Paula Rego* (Phaidon, 2nd, edn, 1997), p.98. Rego turns the angel into a massive and overwhelming Bugs Bunny.

13. For a late example of the same tradition, note how the child is treated in Piero della Francesca's *Nativity* in the National Gallery.

14. Once attributed to St Bonaventure, the work is now thought to have been written in the early 14th century by a Franciscan friar. Its often moving way of expanding upon the gospel story of Jesus' life became hugely popular and influential.

15. The family of James and John have hired servants (Mark 1:20). Ignatius Loyola, unlike the author of the *Meditations*, is among the many who suppose that this was also true of the Holy Family.

16. Quoted without reference in L. Parris, *The Pre-Raphaelites* (Tate, 1973), pp. 9–10.

17. Household Words, 15 June, 1850.

18. John 2:4. Contrast 17:1.

19. For my own attempt to interpret the miracle, see D. Brown, *The Word To Set You Free* (SPCK, 1995), pp. 128–31.

20. Matt. 11:11.

21. John 19:25–7. For a discussion of the possibilities, see R. E. Brown, *The Gospel According to John, XII–XXI* (Anchor Bible, Doubleday, New York, 1970), pp. 922–7.

22. Mark 14:50 and 15:40 (RSV), with parallels in Matthew and Luke. Luke, though, omits the flight of the disciples and adds the presence of 'his acquaintances' to the women viewing from 'afar off' (23:49).

23. Ilustrated in C. Lloyd, *Fra Angelico* (Phaidon, 2nd edn, 1992), no. 48.

24. Very detailed rules for the representation of Mary were given in the influential *El Arte de la Pintura* of Francisco Pacheco (1564–1654).

25. Now in the Kunsthalle, Bremen.

26. In *De Virginitate* Ambrose deduces that the Virgin Mary was, in fact, the first witness to the resurrection.

27. Now in the National Gallery of Victoria, Melbourne.

28. That by Flandes is in the Prado in Madrid, while Schongauer's is at Colmar in France.

29. Isaiah 7:14.

30. Rubens' reputation and popularity have only declined this century, whereas by the 19th century El Greco's work had been relegated to an attic in the Prado. His version of the Assumption which I discuss in the text is now in the Art Institute, Chicago; Rubens' version is in the Maurithuis in The Hague.

31. I pursue these issues in more detail in 'Mary and virgin promise', chapter 5 of my forthcoming book, *Discipleship and Imagination*. (Oxford University Press, 2000).

Reflections on the Iconography of the Virgin as a Figure of Divine Mercy in Medieval Art

Catherine Oakes

In a tract written in praise of the Virgin produced in 12th-century Canterbury, the author made the following pronouncement on the workings of human redemption:

> For because she brought forth Him through whom the dead are made alive and mankind saved from sin, and because no-one can be brought to justice except through Him whom she nurtured in her womb; so there is no salvation except through Him to whom she gave birth.[1]

The passage demonstrates on the one hand the vital link between justice and salvation, and on the other the underpinning of both in the Incarnation. It gives us an insight into a 12th-century perception of the ubiquitous image of the Virgin and Child, and an understanding of the weighty significance of such an image for contemporaries. The Virgin and Child is the visual expression of the Incarnation and therefore of the operation of divine mercy. How the image changed through the medieval centuries reflects the way this doctrine was developed and understood.

The Virgin's perceived power as an intercessor is rooted in her essential role in the Incarnation. If she gave human life to the Redeemer so, in turn, He gave glorified life to her in heaven. Her maternal role was complemented by titles such as Queen and Bride, which emphasized the Virgin's continuing integral role in the ongoing scheme of salvation.[2] As intercessor to her Son in heaven she represented the merciful face of the Divine, in dialogue on behalf of humankind with the just God. From the 12th century there existed a fully developed iconography reflecting these trends. The Virgin appears crowned, her bodily assumption is illustrated, she is represented enthroned with her Son, and she intercedes to Him in scenes of the Last Judgement.[3]

   The foregoing describes two groups of images associated with
the Virgin as a figure of mercy – those which refer to her role in
the Incarnation and those which are related to her role as intercessor. What follows is an attempt to survey, if only briefly, some
of the main developments in medieval Marian iconography in
this area, and to consider how we may approach the meaning of
such images for the people for whom they were made.

   For the 13th-century Bishop of Mende, William Durandus,
there were three ways to depict God – in majesty, on the cross,
and as a child in His mother's lap.[4] Of these the latter is the most
ancient, appearing in 3rd-century catacomb painting.[5] From the
10th century, free-standing cult statues of the Virgin and Child
were widely venerated in European devotion.[6] Typically, early
types of such images, in two and three dimensions, would show a
small but adult Christ blessing with His right hand, seated upon
a rigid and hierarchic representation of the Virgin. No human
relationship is expressed between the two. On the surface it is a
bald statement of Incarnation without any of the implications of
the event expressed in terms of human feeling. For the initiated
observer it may also be redolent of the long-term anticipation of
the birth of Christ in Old Testament prophecy. The Virgin, for
example, is portrayed as a throne upon which her child sits.
Sometimes lions flank the composition, so making explicit the
reference to Solomon's throne and the connection between the
mother and the seat of wisdom, and the Son and the wise king
who sits on it. Frequently Mary carries a flowering stem, referring
to Isaiah's prophecy about Jesse's progeny in which the Virgin,
according to medieval exegesis, was the stem (*virga* as expressed
in the Latin Vulgate) from which the flower which is Christ
grows.[7]

   The headiness of such imagery was gradually replaced from the
second half of the 12th century by representations of the Virgin
and Child in which an affectionate relationship between the two
is expressed. Such a development may have been inspired by an
increasing pre-occupation with the impact of the human nature
of Christ on His experience, reflected too in developments in
Passion iconography.[8] Whatever, one aspect of this development
was that the Virgin and Child, so clearly undifferentiated in early

medieval iconography where the lack of relationship enables them to be represented almost as a fused single composition, becomes an image clearly composed of two individuals engaged in loving dialogue. This is a liberating development in terms of another area of Marian iconography, in which the Virgin has to be shown as functioning as an individual in order to be effective – that is, when she is represented as intercessor. This late medieval type of Virgin and Child does not wholly abandon symbolic references to the special significance of the pair for the sake of realism. Mary frequently by this period wears a crown so that her role as Queen of the glorified Christ is integrated with her maternal role in the one image. Tokens held by one or the other, or aspects of their appearance, may encompass the whole cycle of salvation in their reference. Christ may hold an apple reminiscent of the Fall, or a finch symbolic of the Resurrection, and the Virgin may still hold a flowering stem. The Passion is always anticipated in such images by the cross nimbus around Christ's head.

From the 13th century the Virgin may be shown suckling the Christ child, a development which, as we shall see, was also to have its impact on the iconography of intercession. More generally, the development of Marian imagery often appears to have been shaped by the wider context within which its full significance could be understood. With reference to the types of imagery considered in this article, the development of the so-called *Pietà* from the 14th century, which shows the Virgin cradling the dead, adult Christ in her arms, has such a powerful impact because it echoes the Gothic Virgin and Child image. A remarkable example of this echoing iconography is demonstrated in an early 15th-century diptych from the Netherlands in the Hermitage Museum in St Petersburg. Here the seated Virgin and Child mirrors a *Pietà* on the other panel. It is not, however, the conventional *Pietà*, but a type of Trinity image in which God the Father supports the dead Christ on His lap. So, through a series of iconographic triggers the viewer is led to link the Incarnation with the Passion, the Virgin mother with the heavenly Father, and the human and divine nature of Christ. Similarly the Virgin and St John flanking the enthroned Christ in conventional intercessory imagery is reminiscent of the same pair on either side of the cross. We are led therefore to identify the judge with the man on the cross. The standing Virgin and Child type, which ultimately has its origins in early Byzantine art, was formative in the creation of the scene of the Virgin's Dormition which includes the same image, but represented in reverse – the standing Christ carrying the Virgin's soul, depicted as a baby, in His arms. Thus the Virgin's birth into the glorified life mirrors her Son's incarnation.

Such iconographic cross-referencing must have come naturally to a mindset which experienced religious imagery more regularly and more exclusively than modern society. The same triggering and mirroring devices can also be discerned in the development of formulae representing aspects of the Virgin's intercession. Whilst the Virgin's general powers of intercession were recognized from the early Christian period, the particular location of these powers at the point of death and at the judgement of the soul becomes evident in the 9th and 10th centuries. It is witnessed, for instance, in the wide distribution of the 9th-century miracle story of Theophilus, who sold his soul to the devil and was finally rescued from damnation by the Virgin, and in Anselm's prayer, the *Admonitio Moriendi*, which calls on the Virgin's help at the point of death.[9] This thinking led to iconographic types showing the Virgin interceding to the enthroned Judge for the souls of humankind. The earlier types tend to depict her in the company of another intercessor – often John the Baptist, especially in Byzantine art or, in the West, St Peter.[10] By the late 12th century, however, John the Apostle emerged as the most usual intercessory partner to the Virgin, an early example appearing on the West front of Laon cathedral. Here the Judge raises His hands to show His wounds whilst behind Him angels carry the Instruments of the Passion. The Virgin and John immediately flank Him, the latter, unusually in this context, supporting his head in his hand – a conventional gesture of grief and a posture adopted by John in crucifixion imagery. Whilst this was not to remain a feature of such intercessory iconography, and John was soon to adopt an attitude of prayer like the Virgin, this fleeting detail proves the close influence of the Passion scene on the formation of this iconographic type. The showing of the wounds and the Instruments of the Passion do, on the other hand, remain a fairly constant feature. So we find that mercy is asked from a Judge who is visually identified with the merciful, sacrificed Son. The Virgin elicits mercy from one who is shown to be predisposed to be merciful.

In the later medieval period the Virgin may appear on her own as intercessor or in the company of her wounded Son. In such images figures representing God the Son's human birth and death – the Virgin and the suffering Christ – ask for mercy from the glorified Father. Often it is clear from inscriptions on the image, or the way the figures are arranged, that the Virgin intercedes to the Son and the Son to the Father. This intercessory chain probably derives from a passage in one of St Bernard's Marian sermons which were widely known in the Middle Ages. He advocates that humankind should plead to the Virgin rather than directly to the Son because she is sweet and approachable offering us all, as he endearingly puts it, 'milk and wool'.[11]

The Virgin frequently intercedes with her breast bared. She adopts this posture in intercessory imagery from the second half of the 13th century, a development which occurs in the wake of the appearance of the suckling Virgin and Child type, some 50 or so years before. Indeed, one of its earliest appearances in English art, in a cycle illustrating the Theophilus miracle, shows on one register Theophilus praying to an image of the suckling Virgin on the altar, and on the other the Virgin baring her breast to the glorified Judge, her Son.[12] In this example, through the breast motif, the identity between Judge and the suckling child is underlined. The type appears again at the top of the early 14th-century *Mappa Mundi* in Hereford Cathedral, where an inscription records the Virgin's words to her Son in which she says her gesture is to remind the Judge of His human nature, so that He will show mercy.[13]

The intercessory chain and the exposing of the breast conflate in an image which is described in an early 14th-century Dominican work, the *Speculum Humanae Salvationis*, and which first appears in illustrated manuscripts of the text.[14] In this the Virgin shows her breast to her wounded Son and He, in turn, shows the wound in His side to His Father. Divorced from the text the type is fairly widely distributed in late medieval European art. Once again the image contains an important mirroring mechanism. The Virgin cupping her breast in her hand is reflected by Christ cupping His wound in exactly the same position. As the Virgin nourished Christ, so Christ nourishes humankind with His blood. Further significance can be elicited in the light of the medieval credence that a mother's milk was made from transmuted blood.[15] Thus, the symbol of Christ's human nourishment becomes a mirror for His mortal suffering.

As an image of divine mercy the Virgin may be represented as one who intervenes in the due course of judgement. In such images she effectively stands between the Judge and those about to be judged. She therefore visually represents in a very graphic way a recurring tenet of faith in the Middle Ages, that God's mercy comes before His judgement. It is an idea which appears in the Psalms and is reiterated throughout medieval literature, most famously perhaps in the Franciscan *Dies Irae*.[16] An example of this type of Marian iconography is the so-called Virgin of Mercy, which shows Mary enveloping her devotees under the folds of her cloak, so putting herself, as it were, between her protegées and that from which she is protecting them. When the image appears with naked souls rather than clothed individuals taking shelter, then there is a clear reference to the Virgin's merciful role at the Last Judgement. By no means all of the surviving Virgin of Mercy images fall into this category and some of the most famous, for example the San Sepulchro Madonna by Piero della Francesca, show simply her claimed sponsorship of a particular social group. An individual confraternity may be indicated, for example, by the garments worn.[17]

The Virgin of Mercy is a feature of late medieval art, although as a literary metaphor the image of protection with a shield, or with wings or with a cloak, goes back to the Old Testament.[18] One of the earliest connections made between the Virgin and this protective posture occurs in a 6th-century miracle account, which describes her protecting with her cloak a young Jewish boy, who had been thrown into an oven, from the flames which threatened to engulf him.[19] The iconographic type, however, fully emerged in the 14th century, appearing first, it seems, on Cistercian seals.[20] Whilst it may have emerged in a Cistercian milieu, its dissemination is largely due to its adoption by the Dominicans and its appearance as an illustration in the widely circulated *Speculum Humanae Vitae*, already referred to.

The image is rare in British medieval art. An unusual example survives in a manuscript of Augustine's *Civitate Dei*, which demonstrates the versatility of the iconography to encompass a wide range of meanings. The text is written in a 12th-century hand, but the illuminated initial which introduces it and which includes the Virgin of Mercy was added in the mid-14th century. The composition consists of a conventional Christ in Majesty, showing His wounds and flanked by angels holding the Instruments of the Passion. Below Him, the Virgin stands sheltering numerous naked figures, many of them identified as monks and bishops by tonsures and mitres. It appears therefore that here, at the Apocalypse, the Virgin protects the Church from Christ's judgement. It is not, however, as simple as that. A detail in the image qualifies this reading. The Virgin holds her arms out very straight and, above them, the artist has painted in a sun, to her right, and a moon, to her left. The appearance of the sun and moon in this position had, since the 6th century, been a regular feature of Passion imagery, appearing in this position above the arms of the cross.[21] It seems that again the medieval artist is exploiting the device of mirroring iconography in order to make a visual identity between the mercy of the Mother and that of the Son.

Another point to consider is the context of the illumination. It introduces a work by St Augustine in which the Virgin hardly features. Why then has this image been chosen to accompany such a text? It is possible that the female figure in the image is also to be understood as a personification of the Church. Indeed, the Virgin herself was widely assigned the role of *Ecclesia* in medieval theology.[22] So the Church, the 'City of God' of Augustine's text, here gathers her citizens under her cloak. The Church militant on earth thus appears beneath the Church triumphant, represented by the figure of the glorified Christ in judgement above. As an image in a scholarly book, it might be expected that a number of sophisticated nuances of meaning should be attached to it. There can be no doubt that the Marian reference was intended. Although still in its early stages, the iconography had already been developed as a Marian type both in Italy and Northern Europe by this date. John Grandisson, the Bishop of Exeter, who commissioned (or who was certainly closely associated with) the creation of the image for the manuscript, is well documented as a particular devotee of the Virgin.[23] He had a taste for contemporary Italian art, and was also a benefactor of the Cistercian order in which milieu, as has been shown, the image appears to have first developed in the 14th century.[24] On the one hand, then, the ecclesial interpretation gives us a vision of the City of God, a community governed by justice, mediated by mercy in which the Virgin of Mercy protects, champions and represents the Church. The illumination can also be seen as an image of mercy rooted in the Incarnation in the figure of Mary, the Redemption in the mirroring reference to the cross, and in the merciful judgement at the Apocalypse, to be seen in the figure of Christ and the protecting posture of the Virgin.

A second image in which the Virgin appears to be qualifying the process of justice by her actions is that in which St Michael weighs souls in his scales at the point of judgement. The Virgin interferes by placing her hand or, often in English art, a rosary in the scale pan to favour the fortunes of the soul being weighed. As with the protective cloak, so with the image of weighing in scales, the visual type is rooted in ancient metaphors. In biblical literature it appears, for instance, in the books of Job and Daniel, as well as in the apocryphal book of Esdras.[25] The origins of the iconography of Michael weighing souls (the so-called *Psychostasis*) in the context of the Last Judgement can be found in 11th-century Byzantine art.[26] Certainly by the 12th century the image, either isolated or in this context, was fairly common, especially in French architectural sculpture.[27] By this date also, miracle stories were in circulation in which the Virgin or some other saint interfered with the weighing of a soul as described above.[28] When this variation on the *Psychostasis* theme began to appear in the visual arts in the 14th century, it was almost always the Virgin who appeared as the intervening Saint. The tendency is also reflected in late medieval popular literature. No doubt the appearance of the miracle story in the 13th-century *Legenda Aurea*, in that part of the text written for the Feast of the Assumption, influenced this Marian development.[29]

An example appearing on a painted vault in the church at Fanefjord in Denmark, dating from the mid 15th century, shows a version of the miracle which is distinct in some features from the normal type to be found in English art. Here it is not just the Virgin, but the Virgin and Child, who interfere with St Michael's scales. As in the *Legenda Aurea* account, so here, the Virgin places her hand on the scale beam. The rosary is not included. The context of this image is also of interest. It appears on a quadripartite vault, placed opposite a depiction of the Sacrifice of Isaac. The angel, raising his hand to stop Abraham's slaughter of his son, is reflected in the Virgin raising her hand to intervene with the weighing process. As divine mercy qualifies divine justice in the story of Isaac, so it does in the interference with the scales. Significantly, the traditional New Testament counterpart in medieval iconography for the Sacrifice of Isaac is the Crucifixion. The presence of the baby, cross-nimbussed Christ in the Fanefjord version of the Marian *Psychostasis* has already been noted, and Durandus' description of the images of God, which includes both Christ on the cross and in His mother's arms. A third consideration in the interpretation of this image is a late medieval iconographic formula, influenced by early theological metaphors, in which the cross itself represents the scales upon which human sin is weighed and redeemed by the counter-balance of Christ's suffering in the other scale-pan.[30] So again, metaphors of mercy – the Virgin and Child and the reference to the Crucifixion – are blended with a metaphor of judgement – the scales. Clearly, the imagery and literature available in the late middle ages, even at a parochial level, as at the little church of Fanefjord, interrelated and synergetically produced a rich understanding of the mechanisms of medieval teaching on human salvation.

This paper has attempted, in summary form, to highlight Marian images representing divine mercy in medieval iconography. Two main categories have been considered – types which represent the Incarnation and those which represent the Virgin's intercession. In both cases it has been argued that the full significance of the Virgin's role can only be understood in the context of her partnership with Christ – as her child, her suffering Son, her heavenly Father, her celestial bridegroom, and glorified judge. The awareness of this rich nexus of relationships influenced the development of the iconography and informed its meaning for contemporaries. The result was a brilliant visual commentary on the workings of divine justice in relationship with divine mercy, either understood by the intellectual minority in its rich complexity, or apprehended by the majority more simply, as the Virgin herself understood it:

And His mercy is on them that fear Him.[31]

Notes

1. William of Malmesbury, *De IV Virtutibus B. Mariae, Patrologia cursus compleus: series latina*, ed. J.-P. Migne, 162 vols. (Paris: Migne, etc., 1857–1866), 159, col. 586. Author's translation.

2. She was already being addressed as Queen of Heaven by the end of the Patriarchal period. See H. Graef, *Mary: A History of Doctrine and Devotion*, 2 vols (London: Sheed & Ward, 1963, 1965; repr. in one vol. 1985), p. 155 & pp.160–1. The link between Queenship and intercession was to be explicitly made in the original form of the *Salve Regina*, addressed to *Regina Misericordiae* and in the Marian antiphon, *Ave Regina Coelorum*, which finishes with a plea for intercession. Both were probably composed in the 11th century. M. Britt, *The Hymns of the Breviary and the Missal* (New York: Benziger Bros Inc., 1948), pp. 66–7. For the Virgin as *Sponsa*, see M. O'Carroll, *Theotokos: A Theological Encyclopaedia of the Blessed Virgin Mary*, revised edition (Wilmington, Delaware: Michael Glazier, Inc., 1983), pp. 333–4. The epithet was also linked to Marian commentaries on the Song of Songs. See D. Turner, *Eros and Allegory: Medieval Exegesis of the Song of Songs in the High Middle Ages*, Cistercian studies series no.156 (Kalamazoo, 1995) and R. Lee Fulton, *The Virgin Mary and the Song of Songs in the High Middle Ages* (unpublished doctoral thesis, Columbia University, 1994).

3. Whilst not a feature of Byzantine iconography, in the West the Virgin appears crowned, or about to be crowned, by the 10th century. See, for example, the Dormition of the Virgin in the 10th-century Benedictional of St Aethelwold from Winchester (London, British Library, Add. ms 49598), and an Anglo-Saxon ivory panel depicting the Last Judgement dating from the late 10th or early 11th century, now in the Museum of Archaeology and Ethnography in Cambridge. The earliest surviving image of the Assumption is on a Byzantine

textile fragment dating from the 8th century, now in Sens Cathedral Treasury. The mosaic in the apse of Sta Maria Trastevere in Rome is decorated with an early example of the Virgin enthroned with Christ dating from the first half of the 12th century. Both figures carry texts derived from the Song of Songs which had been incorporated into Assumption liturgy. The ivory panel in Cambridge already referred to shows an early Western example of the Virgin interceding to the Judge. The so-called *Deesis* group, featuring the Virgin and John the Baptist interceding to Christ, but not explicitly in a Last Judgement context, was developed in the Greek world in the 9th and 10th centuries.

4. William Durandus, '*Rationale Divinorum Officiorum*', eds, A. Davril and T.M. Thoibodeau, *Corpus Christianorum* 140 (Turnhout: Brepols, 1995), p.37.

5. There are two images of a mother suckling a child in the catacombs of Priscilla, dating from the 3rd and 4th centuries. One, and probably both, represent the Virgin and Child.

6. The earliest documented free-standing image of the Virgin and Child of any size was that made for the Cathedral of Clermont-Ferrand by the goldsmith Aleaume, in the mid 10th century. A late-10th-century drawing of it survives in a manuscript now in the municipal library at Clermont-Ferrand.

7. Isaiah 11:1.

8. Literature such as the Franciscan mid-13th-century lyric, *Stabat Mater*, and Pseudo-Bonaventure's late-13th/early-14th century *Meditationes Vitae Christi* reflect this development. For Passion iconography in the West see G. Schiller, *Ikonographie der christlichen Kunst*, 5 vols (Gutersloh: Gutersloher Verlagshaus Gerd Mohn, 1996–1991), trans. J. Seligman, vols 1 and 2 (London: Lund Humphries, 1971 and 1972), vol. 2, pp. 9–12, and 88–161.

9. For Theophilus, see O'Carroll (1983), pp. 341–2. For the *Admonitio Moriendi* and similar prayers see R. Woolf, *The English Lyric in the Middle Ages* (Oxford: Oxford University Press, 1968), pp. 119–22.

10. John the Baptist appears, for instance, on a group of 10th-century Byzantine ivories depicting the *Deesis* now in the Louvre, Paris, and in the Palazzo Venezia, Rome. Peter accompanies the Virgin Mary as intercessor in the Cambridge ivory mentioned above, and on the 12th-century West tympanum of Ste Foy at Conques (Rouergue). See also the Romanesque painted 'coelum' at Kempley (Herefordshire) and wall-paintings at Asnières-sur-Veyre (Maine).

11. *Sancti Bernardi Opera*, eds, J. Leclercq and H. Rochais, 8 vols (Rome: Editiones Cistercienses, 1957–1977), vol. 5 (1968), p.263.

12. The Lambeth Apocalypse, London, Lambeth Palace, ms 209, fol. 46v.

13. The French inscription translates: 'Here, my dear Son, my bosom is whence You took flesh/ Here are my breasts from which You sought a Virgin's milk/ Show pity, as You said You would, on all/ Who their devotion paid to me for You have made me Saviouress.' See A. L. Moir, *The World Map in Hereford Cathedral* (Hereford Cathedral, 1970), p.11.

14. For a late medieval printed illustrated example see *The Mirour of Mans Salvacioune: A middle english translation of Speculum Humanae Salvationis*, ed. A. Henry (Aldershot: Scolar Press, 1986).

15. See C.W. Bynum, *Jesus as Mother, Studies in the Spirituality of the High Middle Ages* (Berkeley: University of California Press, 1982), pp. 132–3. The belief is also significant in the light of the story of the pelican pecking at her breast to

feed her young with her blood, which appears in the Bestiary and symbolizes Christ's sacrifice for humankind.

16. See F.J.E. Raby, *A History of Christian-Latin Poetry from the beginnings to the close of the Middle Ages*, 2nd edn (Oxford: Clarendon Press, 1953), p. 448.

17. See, for example, a confraternity of flagellants protected by the Virgin's cloak in an early-15th-century painting by Pietro di Domenico da Monte Pulciano, now in Avignon.

18. The metaphor appears in the latin Vulgate, for instance, in Psalms 17:8, 36:7, 57:1, 61:4, 63:7 and 91:4.

19. The origins and variations of this widely circulated legend are surveyed in *The Stella Maris of John of Garland*, ed. E.F. Wilson (Cambridge, Mass: The Medieval Academy of America, 1946), pp. 157–9.

20. See P. Perdrizet, *La Vièrge de Misèricorde. Étude d'un Thème Iconographique* (Paris: A. Fontemoing, 1908), chapter 2. This is the pioneering work on the image, although some of Perdrizet's conclusions have been challenged by more recent writers. For a relatively up-to-date bibliography see A. Thomas, 'Schutzmantelmaria', in *Die Gottesmutter: Marienbild in Rheinland und in Westfalen. Herausgegeben von Leonhard Kuppers* (Recklinghausen: Aurel Bongers, 1974).

21. See Schiller, vol. 2 (1972), figs.32 and 331.

22. For a discussion of the identity between the Virgin and Ecclesia in medieval theology and iconography, see P. Verdier, *Le Couronnement de la Vièrge: les origines et les premiers développements d'un thème iconographique* (Montreal: Institut d'Études Médiévales, 1980).

23. See N. Orme, *Exeter Cathedral 1050–1550* (Exeter: Devon Books, 1986), pp. 85–6. Also, J. Cherry, 'The Ring of Bishop Grandisson', in *Medieval Art and Architecture at Exeter Cathedral. Conference Transactions of the British Archaeological Association for 1985*, ed. F. Kelly (1991), 205–9. The two rings of Grandisson which have survived both carry depictions of the Virgin and Child. The inscription on one of them reads, *Ego sum Mater Misericordi(a)e.*

24. Grandisson gave a copy of Eadmer's writings to the Cistercian community at Abbey Dore. See N.R. Ker, *Medieval Libraries of Great Britain: a list of surviving books*, 2nd edn (London: Royal Historical Society, 1964), pp. 81–5.

25. Job 31:16, Daniel 5:27 and Esdras Bk 4, 3:34.

26. For example in Paris, Bibliotheque Nationale, ms grec. 74, fol. 51v.

27. See, for example, at Saintes, St Eutrope – capital in crypt; Conques (Rouergue) – west tympanum; Corme-Royale (Saintonge) – corbel on west front; Autun, Cathedral of St Lazaire – west tympanum.

28. A *Psychostasis* with St Lawrence intervening, for example, is referred to by G. Philippart in 'Le Recit Miraculaire Marial dans l'Occident Medievale', in *Marie: Le Culte de la Vièrge dans la Societé Médiévale* (Paris: Beauchésne, 1996), p.575.

29. James of Voragine, *Legenda Aurea*, ed. T. Graesse, (Osnabruck: Otto Zeller Verlag, 1969), p.515.

30. See F. Wormald, 'The Crucifix and the Balance', *Journal of the Warburg and Courtauld Institutes* 1 (1937/8), 276–80.

31. Luke 1:50.

Guardians of the Way

Sarah Jane Boss

A collector of Scottish folklore, F. Marian McNeill, recorded the following information in the 1950s:

> A charm still used in the Hebrides is the *Airne Mhoire* (literally, the kidney of Mary), or the Virgin's Nut, on which the mark of a cross is faintly discernible. These seeds are carried across the Atlantic by the Gulf Stream and are occasionally cast up on the shore. Being rare, they are highly prized. In the Roman Catholic islands they are often blest by the priest. The charm is used by women in childbed, the midwife placing it in the hand of the expectant mother, who clasps it tight in the belief that it will ease her pain and ensure a safe delivery.

McNeill vividly brings this account to life with the following anecdote:

> A friend of the present writer's, a Roman Catholic, who lives in the Hebrides, has in her possession a Virgin's Nut on which a small silver cross has been mounted, and which has been blessed by a former bishop of the diocese. Late one evening, in 1936, a young man arrived breathless at her door and begged her to lend him the nut. His wife was expecting her first child and was already in labour; a friend of his had lost his wife in similar circumstances and he was resolved to take no risks. The nut was safely returned with the news that all had gone well.[1]

The belief that Mary is a powerful protectress of women in labour has been widespread in Western Europe. In Medieval England, for example, women who went to be churched after child-bearing would say a prayer of thanksgiving for their safe delivery and light a candle in front of the Lady altar. The great mystic Bridget of

Sweden was the mother of eight children, and it is reputed that when she was undergoing an extremely difficult labour, the Virgin Mary herself came to the bedside. The Blessed Virgin eased Bridget's sickness and ensured that she was safely delivered of her child.

Child-bearing is, of course, an occasion of great danger: it is a time when the life and health of both mother and child are at risk. It is not surprising, therefore, that in many cultures across the world women seek supernatural assistance to support and guard them through this period, subject as they are to natural forces of life and death. Within Christianity, supernatural assistance of this kind has been sought from a variety of different saints; but most commonly, it is the Virgin Mary who is invoked to give succour to women in childbed. This is partly because she is believed to be the most powerful of all the saints, so that people frequently appeal to her in their greatest extremities. But in addition to this, Mary gives special protection to women in labour because, according to legend and tradition, she herself gave birth without suffering pain or injury. Having accomplished the birth of her own son without enduring any hardship, Mary has been a deep source of encouragement to women who are hoping that they too will be spared the sickness which so often attends parturition, and who pray that their children, like Mary's, will be born alive and well.

In Toulouse, in Southern France, the black Virgin called Notre-Dame-de-la-Daurade used also to be known as *Notre-Dame-de-Bonne-Couches* – 'Our Lady of Good Childbirth'. The Virgin has a sash which the church lends out to ease the pains of women in labour. It is the custom for mothers to borrow the sash to give to their daughters during childbirth, just as their own mothers have done for them in the past. The tradition is thus handed down from one generation to the next.

Yet childbirth is not only a time of physical danger; it is also a state of *transition*: a woman becomes a mother; a community receives a new member; a new infant passes through the bounds of a human body as it moves from the womb to the outside world; and the mother's own body reverts from pregnancy to its former condition.

This, however, is only one of many dangerous periods of transition which human beings have to undergo. Sometimes these transitions involve obvious danger to people's physical well-being; this is the case not only with childbirth, but also, for example, with a sea-voyage, or recovery from a serious illness. In other instances, the immediate danger seems to be more spiritual than physical. Thus, in many societies the change from one stage of life to another, e.g., from childhood to adulthood, is guarded about by elaborate rituals. These are designed to keep away evil influences and to encourage a smooth passage from one state to the next. The most striking examples of this kind of ritual are perhaps those associated with death – which is, after all, the most decisive of all points of transition. In this connection, one might call to mind the English custom of opening all the windows when somebody has died, 'so that the soul can escape easily'; or of covering mirrors, so that the departing soul does not get mixed up with reflections which would inadvertently bind it back within the world of the living.

Periods of transition, then, appear to be especially dangerous – especially vulnerable to mishap – and therefore in special need of protection. And the rituals, legends and sacred sites associated with black Virgins indicate that these numinous figures are frequently considered to be the powerful guardians of transitional times.

It is possible that the attribution of this general power may derive from a black Virgin's particular role as protectress of women in labour. This has been suggested by the French Benedictine Dom Jacques de Bascher, in his history of the Black Virgin of Paris. This large, miracle-working statue is known as *Notre-Dame de Bonne Délivrance*, 'Our Lady of Safe Deliverance', and this is usually understood as a reference to the Virgin's reputation for releasing prisoners. However, de Bascher puts forward an alternative suggestion to account for the title:

It is always asserted that the pilgrims and devotees of ancient times attributed Black Virgins with a very special power when it came to anything connected with fertility: to Black Virgins married women would address their prayers to obtain the gift of a child, and mothers who were close to term would seek the benefit of a happy delivery. Subsequently, this 'speciality' was extended to other 'deliveries': to that of prisoners for example, and eventually to every kind of necessity and distress.[2]

This, suggests de Bascher, is the probable origin of the title *Notre-Dame de Bonne Délivrance*.

This is a claim which is rather hard to substantiate. Nevertheless, we shall see that the safe deliverance of souls during periods of perilous transition is indeed a particular concern of many black Virgins. Moreover, there are good poetic reasons why people have used the metaphor of child-bearing to help understand these journeys of spiritual danger. Parturition is a time of acute pain and total disablement; but it results in the miracle of a precious new life.

Yet it is not only times but also places, which can be points of transition; and these spatial 'places of passage' seem to stand just as much in need of ritual protection as do the temporal periods of change which have been mentioned above.

Crossroads, for example, are points of intersection which can signify transition of more than one kind. They often mark the crossing of a boundary between two different territories; but in Celtic folklore they can also provide the site for transition between the day-to-day world of things which are earthly, and the 'other' world of spirits and fairy-folk. A transition of just this kind occurs in the Scottish ballad *Tam-Lin*. The enchanted knight, Tam-Lin, has been captured by the otherworldly Queen of the Fairies, and he is rescued from her clutches only when his earthly lover, Janet, seizes him at 'Miles Cross' on Hallowe'en.

Crossroads were also traditional places for hanging criminals and burying suicides. This might have been intended to ensure that the victims' souls would linger at the crossroads to guard the way; or it might have been the remnant of some ancient practice in which human sacrifices were offered to a guardian deity.

Horseshoes and other lucky charms attached to doors and lintels express a concern with points of transition, since the talisman serves to guard the threshold of a house, and thus to protect the passage of entry. This keeps any evil influences from reaching the interior of the building.

Black Virgins frequently appear to be guardians of places of passage: places where two worlds meet, and where there is movement from one to the other. Places of physical passage are also sites of spiritual transition, and black Virgins protect the way both literally and metaphorically.

In the Hollow of the Rock

Of all the sites which are sacred to a black Virgin, one of the greatest is at Rocamadour in south-western France. The river Alzou has cut a vast gorge through the grey limestone of the Cause de Quercy, and the Medieval buildings of the little shrine-town are built onto the side of the south-facing cliff of the river valley (Fig.1). There is a ledge on the cliff, which is a natural formation against the rock face and, according to legend, it was upon this ledge that a hermit named Amadour came to live his life of solitude. He is said to have built an oratory here in honour of the Virgin, and there was also a spring which rose nearby. In the 12th century, a tomb was discovered in the rock, close to the entrance to the Virgin's chapel, and the body within the tomb was believed to be that of St Amadour. It was duly exhumed and placed inside the chapel, where it remained until the chapel was destroyed by Huguenots in the 16th century.

The name Amadour means 'lover', and it is variously interpreted to mean such things as 'lover of God' or 'lover of the rock'. Rocamadour is popularly said to be named after the saint: it is Amadour's Rock. Nevertheless, the prodigious number of miracles associated with the holy site are all attributed to the Virgin, and it is to her that pilgrimage here has always been made.

In some versions of the legend, Amadour is said to have been a servant in the household of Jesus and Mary, and to have brought the statue of the Virgin and Child from the Holy Land. However, the traditions of devotion at Rocamadour seem to be more concerned with the sanctity of the place itself than with the narratives about Amadour which have accumulated over the centuries. The holiness of the site undoubtedly resides in 'the cleft in the rock' – 'the shelter under the rock'. Indeed, one wall of the Virgin's chapel consists simply of the unworked cliff face.

There is at present no archaeological or textual evidence to indicate that Rocamadour was a sacred site before the advent of Christianity. But excavations along the Alzou valley and surrounding countryside indicate that there was probably continuous occupation of the area for 10,000 years during the later Stone Age and early Iron Age, so it is not by any means impossible that the cult of the Virgin Mary has supplanted more ancient devotions. Furthermore, there is a local tradition which states that there was indeed religious worship at Rocamadour before the Christian founder induced the conversion to his own religion. An English visitor, Frances Gostling, published in 1911 an account of her visit to the shrine. Mrs. Gostling's record contains the information that Druids used to offer human sacrifices there 'to the mysterious Black Mother Soulivia, who reigned in the cavern temple half way up the rock'. Mrs Gostling also recounts a belief concerning the character of the altar in the Virgin's Chapel. 'Today,' she writes, 'it is enclosed and concealed in an outer covering of bronze. But beneath the casing is a very old stone altar, with no place for relics, only a hole, a sort of drain, through which, before the time of the gentle Amadour, the blood of the human sacrifices offered to the goddess Soulivia used to run.'[3]

Emile Saillens points out that the name *Soulivia* is strikingly similar to that of the *Suleviae*, a trinity of female deities known to have been worshipped at Romano-Celtic sites in Northern Europe. In fact, the singular form *Sulevia* is also found in inscriptions, and many Celtic goddesses can appear in both singular and triple form. Saillens states that the Suleviae were sometimes venerated as goddesses of uncultivated land; and this, indeed, is a very apt association for a sanctuary situated on the barren and desolate Causse de Quercy.[4] Of course, land which is uncultivated is sometimes referred to as 'virgin'. But deities can synthesize within themselves stages of life and states of being which could not co-exist on the purely human plane. And so it is that the Romans could render the Suleviae an equivalent of their own virginal Minerva, whilst the three figures were at the same time represented with the attributes of motherhood.

Being a trinity, the Suleviae were apparently identified with the Matronae, the great Mothers who seem to have been the most popular object of unviversal devotion in pre-Christian Britain and Gaul. This in turn raises a speculation as to the possible etymology of the name *Rocamadour*. Most scholars believe the name to be far older than the story contained in the Medieval narrative of Amadour and his rock. They do not, however, agree as to what the origin of the name actually is. One widely held opinion is that Rocamadour is partially formed from the word *roca*, which is a pre-Celtic toponym, i.e., a place name whose origin and meaning is older than the time when Gaul was settled by people who spoke a Celtic language. However, it is not known what *roca* means, and in any case, this account leaves the remainder of the word, *-madour*, entirely unexplained. Yet is it not possible that this part of the name is cognate with the many Indo-European words for 'mother', such as the German 'mutter', the Greek 'mētēr', the Latin 'mater', or its Spanish derivative 'madre'?

Welsh mythology retains traces of an extremely ancient cult of a goddess known as Modron, whose name, like the Latin Matrona, means simply 'mother'. She was honoured together with her son, Mabon, whose name correspondingly means 'son' or 'young man'. At Rocamadour, the cult of a divine Mother and her divine Son could have provided the foundation which, after the incursion of Christianity, would have made the sanctuary well suited for rededication to the Mother of God and her own divine Son.

In ancient times, there was also a spring which rose in the cliff at Rocamadour. And the Celts' extensive devotion to maternal deities overlaps with cults of sacred springs and wells. The Matronae are often depicted bearing the produce of the earth, such as fruits and cereals; and it may be because springs likewise rise up from within the belly of the earth that they too appear to be the bounty of a nurturing mother. At any rate, it is certainly the case that many holy wells were dedicated to a divine Mother or Mothers. At Bath, the great shrine of the goddess Sulis centred on the healing waters of the hot springs.

Among the powers attributed to black Virgins, the ability to bestow fertility and to protect women in labour is quite common.

The shrines of Our Lady of Loreto (Ancona) and Our Lady of Montserrat (Catalonia), are among the most famous of Christian holy places connected with conception and childbirth, but the same power is also said to belong to black Virgins who are quite obscure. When Frances Gostling visited the parish church of Montferrand (at Clermont-Ferrand), she found in one of the side-chapels 'a tiny black antique statue of the Virgin'. Mrs Gostling thought it looked rather neglected, and she commented: 'Only the poorest and humblest of women come to kneel before the little shrine.' But the woman who was dusting the altar on which the statue stood, said that the figure was still 'good for giving children'.[5]

At Rocamadour, Mrs Gostling was told of a custom which suggests that in the past, fertility was a significant motif among the popular traditions at this shrine as well. Roland's sword, Durandal, is stuck into the rock above the Virgin's Chapel, and an old priest, who had visited the place often, told Mrs Gostling 'that it was still the custom of young girls to come with their fiancés and try to pull the sword out of the wall. "If they succeed, it means they will be married within the year," said he with a smile'.[6]

Fruit, crops and springs of clear water are delivered from the womb of the earth to the world of human habitation, and in moving from the realm of dark obscurity to the light of day they seem to move between two worlds – from the shadowy, unknown world of divine origins, to the ordinary sphere of the mundane and familiar. Many sacred sites are places at which these two worlds are believed to meet. In fact, some anthropologists would claim that the function of holy places and rituals is precisely to lead people onto, and even across, the threshold between the mundane and the eternal. In the mythology and religious practice of the Celtic peoples, a concern with movement between the two worlds is strongly marked. The two great festivals of May Eve and Hallowe'en (Samhain and Beltane), for example, mark the transition from one season to another – from winter to summer, and summer to winter; but they are also occasions on which the inhabitants of the Otherworld, the Fairy-folk, are abroad on Earth and contact between the two worlds can easily be made.

This is why it is on Hallowe'en that Tam-Lin can be rescued from the Queen of Fairies. It is also why the Christian Church chose to commemorate All Saints and All Souls at this time of year.

However, there are not only times, but also places, at which the two worlds meet, and there are certain topographical features which seem particularly likely to provide the threshold upon which human beings can encounter the divine. Thus, the Romans often regarded hill-tops as being the particular domain of the god Mercury. This was the case at Mont-Saint-Michel in Brittany, and at the Puy-de-Dôme, which overlooks the Celtic city of Clermont. In both cases, Christians rededicated the sites to St Michael.

Rocks and springs, on the other hand, have commonly been associated with female figures, such as the goddess Sulis at Bath. Indeed, the Roman name for Bath was *Aquae Sulis*: 'the Waters of Sulis'. The meaning of the name *Sulis* is disputed, but it is possible that it is derived from a Celtic root *suil*, meaning 'gap' or 'orifice', implying that the deity is primarily linked to this opening between the two worlds.

A number of black Virgins are worshipped in underground crypts, which are rather like artificial caves. At Chartres, there is the shrine of 'Our Lady of the Crypt', where there is also a well. Similarly, at Clermont-Ferrand, the image of Notre-Dame du Port has always been housed in the crypt, and here also, there is a sacred spring, which rises in front of her altar. It is in this spring that the statue of the black Virgin is reputed to have been discovered.

The religion practised at Rocamadour is likewise the cult of a particular place with its own distinctive geography. Even today, the prayer booklets which are officially produced for use at the shrine contain the invocation: 'Marie, dans le creux du rocher', meaning 'Mary, in the hollow of the rock'. The Suleviae, or Sulevia, who was possibly Rocamadour's previous patroness, has a name which appears to contain the same element, *sul*, as appears in the titular deity of Aquae Sulis. The origins of this name, as mentioned above are obscure, and it is possible that it dates from a time even before the coming of the Celtic peoples to

Northern Europe. But it is undoubtedly the case that pre-Christian peoples considered the sheltering hollows of awe-inspiring cliffs to be places of great sanctity. It is also the case that Rocamadour continues to impress a sense of deep holiness upon its visitors down to the present day.

Rocamadour is truly a place where two worlds meet. At one time, realization of this truth might have been expressed in the language of Celtic myth, but over the centuries it has been re-iterated in the language and imagery of Christian doctrine. For Christian devotion to the Virgin Mary is founded upon the belief that God and humanity were perfectly united in the person of Christ, and that this union occurred when Jesus was conceived in Mary's womb.

Luke's Gospel tells the story of the Angel Gabriel's annuncia-tion to Mary, when, according to Christian tradition, salvation first entered the world (Luke 1:26–38). Ever since Adam and Eve disobeyed God by eating the forbidden fruit in the Garden of Eden, humanity had been estranged from God by sin. But now, at last, it was to be restored to righteousness by the saving work of Christ. In the beginning, God had created Heaven and Earth so that all things were in their proper relationships, both to one another and to their Maker. But, according to the Christian interpretation of Genesis Chapter 3, Adam and Eve wilfully disrupted their harmonious relationship with God, in conse-quence of which all human relationships were rendered difficult and filled with strife: relations between men and women, the rela-tionship of humanity to other animals, and humanity's relation-ship even to the earth itself. Indeed, the waywardness of Adam and Eve introduced the possibility of everlasting death as the final destiny for the human race. Yet God still loved his creation and wished to restore it to its original state of blessedness. In order to accomplish this end, the immortal God humbled himself to become incarnate in human flesh, in the man Jesus Christ: he accepted mortality, and died by crucifixion. But he rose again from the dead on the third day, and by submitting himself to death and being raised from the grave, Christ atoned for the sin which had separated humanity from God, and on behalf of all creation, he overcame death.

During the rite of the Mass, the drama of the Incarnation is symbolically re-enacted. The priest or deacon mixes a little water with the wine which is to be consecrated. The wine signifies divinity, and the water humanity and, as the priest or deacon mixes them, he says: 'By the mystery of this water and wine may we come to share in the divinity of Christ, who humbled himself to share in our humanity.' The uniting of the human and divine natures in Christ makes it again possible for men and women to participate in the divine life of the Godhead. This meeting of Heaven and Earth is lived anew at every celebration of the Mass; but its first and definitive enactment took place in the womb of the Virgin Mary. In fact, the Church Fathers sometimes refer to Mary's womb as the bridal chamber in which God and humanity were wedded to one another, since it was here that the union of the two was consummated.

So Mary is the woman in whom Heaven and Earth found their meeting-place. Hence, it is more than fitting that she should be the guardian of a sacred shrine such as Rocamadour, for the entire significance of this place is tied to the experience of communion and exchange between the divine and the earthly.

The stature of Our Lady of Rocamadour, like the majority of black statues of the Virgin, represents Christian belief in the Incarnation. It is of a type known as the Virgin in Majesty, and was probably carved in the 12th century (Fig.2). Mary is seated upon a throne, and Christ is sitting on her left knee. He was once holding a book in his left hand, although most of this has now been lost. His right hand has also disappeared, but it might once have been formed to carry some kind of sceptre (Fig.3). The heads of both Virgin and Child have been carved with a ridge around them so that they can wear crowns. Christ is depicted not as a baby, but as a small adult, or a child with adult features. Taken together with the insignia of authority, this indicates that Christ is the Son of God, the eternal Word, through whom the Universe was created. At the same time, however, he is only a small child, seated on his mother's knee, and with bare feet. This tells us that he is also a weak human being – a dependent child in need of a mother's support. The statue thus shows Christ as both

God and man: authoritative and vulnerable, Creator and creature. Mary is correspondingly shown to be the Mother of God. She is a human woman who carried the Creator of the Cosmos in her womb, and in her lap.

Like her Son, Mary is crowned and enthroned. There are several ways of interpreting her regal status, but in this instance the most important meaning is that she conceived and bore the ruler of the Universe. In consequence of this, the whole world has been saved from perdition and has the opportunity of attaining Heaven. Mary is therefore honoured above all the angels and saints, and hence becomes the Queen of Heaven and Earth.

Bishop Gregory of Nyssa, in the 4th century, wrote a homily on the Annunciation. In this work, he eloquently conveys a sense of the dignity which is accorded to Mary on account of her being the earthly shrine in which divinity has come to dwell:

> The Lord is with you!
> He is in you and in every place,
> he is with you and of you . . .
> The Son in the bosom of his Father,
> the Only Begotten Son in your womb,
> the Lord, in the way known alone to him,
> all in everyone
> and all in you!
> Blessed are you among women!
> For you have been placed above all virgins,
> for you have been found worthy
> to give shelter to the Lord,
> for you have received within you the One who is so great
> that nothing in the world could him contain,
> you have received him who fills all with himself,
> for you have become the place
> in which has come to pass salvation,
> for you have been the vehicle that has ushered in
> the King to life,
> for you have appeared as a treasure, a spiritual pearl.
> Blessed are you among women![7]

This is surely the insight which underlies devotion to the black Virgin of Rocamadour.

Star of the Sea

Our Lady of Rocamadour is particularly renowned for protecting sailors who are in danger at sea. From one point of view, this does not seem surprising, since Mary has been known by the title *Stella Maris*, 'Star of the Sea', since at least as early as the 7th century. Indeed, throughout Catholic Christianity Mary is regarded as the special protectress of seafarers. For this reason, many sea ports have Marian shrines. Rocamadour, however, is nowhere near the sea. Yet in the Virgin's Chapel at Rocamadour there hangs a miraculous bell which, it is said, sometimes rings of its own accord. When this happens, it signifies that Our Lady of Rocamadour is answering the prayers of seafarers who are calling upon her to deliver them from danger. Over the centuries, many of the miracles which are said to have been worked by Our Lady of Rocamadour consist of the rescuing of voyagers who are caught in storms at sea. People who have been saved in this way have often given votive offerings in the form of model ships, to hang in the Virgin's chapel.

Yet in this respect, Rocamadour does not seem to be alone. For among the sites of devotion to black Virgins, there are others which are situated inland but which, nonetheless, have cultic associations with the sea.

At Orcival, for example, in the diocese of Clermont, there used to be model ships hanging up as votive offerings from sailors who had been rescued. The shrine also has a tradition of singing the hymn *Ave Maris Stella*. This supremely beautiful chant probably dates back to the 8th century, and has always been one of the most popular of Marian hymns. It addresses Mary immediately as 'Star of the Sea', and has therefore tended to be associated with intercession for seafarers. At Orcival, the *Ave Maris* is sung on the Eve of the Ascension, which is Orcival's principal feast day. On this occasion, the statue of the Virgin is carried in procession along a time-honoured route, and it is during this procession that the hymn is sung.[8]

The words of the *Ave Maris* may, in fact, provide a clue to the riddle of why it is that a landlocked sanctuary should be the site of special intercession for sailors. The words of the first verse are as follows:

Ave, maris stella,	Hail, star of the sea,
Dei mater alma,	gracious mother of God,
atque semper virgo,	and perpetual virgin,
felix coeli porta.	fruitful gate of heaven.

All the imagery in theses lines is concerned with the meeting of two worlds – with the union of Heaven and Earth. Mary is the 'Mother of God' and the 'Gate of Heaven'. That is to say, she is the place at which Heaven has come to meet Earth, so that Earth-dwellers might, in turn, be able to enter Heaven. Furthermore, she is both mother and virgin – two states which are normally incompatible with one another. But they are brought together in Mary and thereby suggest the mysterious and incomprehensible bonding of time with eternity. The paradox of the virginal motherhood gives merely a hint that within this woman's body, infinity has dwelt within space. It is here that God and humanity have been miraculously made one.

This points to the significance of the symbol of the sea. To cross the sea is to travel from one land to another; it is to travel to a destination which may not come within sight for many days; and it carries the risks of being shipwrecked, or of being becalmed without adequate provisions. The sea therefore is one of the most powerful symbols for places and times of transition. In the Welsh stories of the *Mabinogion*, the sea often seems to constitute a realm between this earthly world and the supernatural 'other' world. Journeys and meetings between the two worlds take place across the sea. In the symbolism of Christianity, Mary is the guardian of the seas because she is the channel by which God came to be united with his creation. It is by passing through her that the divine and the earthly come to embrace.

In the days before magnetic compasses, the 'star of the sea' was a name for the lode-star. This was the fixed star which sailors used to guide them across the ocean. Mary, *Stella Maris*, is thus the lode-star who saves her devotees from getting lost in times and places of transition; she is the port through whom the earthly pilgrim enters Heaven in safety.

Rocamadour, like other shrines of black Virgins, is a place where Earth meets Heaven and where the passage between the two is open. The sea signifies this place of crossing, and the Virgin Mother is the powerful guardian of both the rock and the ocean. She is the protectress of those who undertake perilous journeys.

Crossing the Boundary

In Classical antiquity, places of transition were often guarded by the goddess Hecate. It was common for an upright stone to be dedicated to Hecate and placed near a doorway. On the last night before the new moon – that is, at the turning point between one month and the next – people would take eggs and fish to crossroads and leave them there as offerings for her.

There were many Classical influences upon the popular culture of South-Eastern Gaul, which is also the area in which black Virgins are most numerous. Marseilles was a Greek colony, founded by Phoceans in about 600 BCE. Centuries later, Roman practices spread through this part of Gaul when it was incorporated into the Roman Empire during the last quarter of the second century BCE. In many places, the old Celtic beliefs and practices were simply overlaid or combined with the newer, imported customs from the cultures of Greece and Rome.

Several sites of black Virgins show signs that they were formerly dedicated to Hecate. Perhaps the most striking example of this is near the town of Noves, which is on the banks of the River Durance in Provence. Noves is situated on an old Roman road, and at the top of a neighbouring hill this route crosses another track which leads from the Camargue to the Alps. A pagan temple was built at the crossroads, facing a spring. In Christian times, this site came to be occupied by the shrine of a black Virgin, one of whose titles was *Notre-Dame des Oeufs*, or 'Our Lady of the Eggs'.[9] This designation derived from the annual custom of leaving eggs for her at the crossroads. Saillens observes that in ancient times it was not only Hecate who received offerings of eggs. He writes: 'The Gallo-Romans also had countryside goddesses called *Comedovae*, "egg-eaters".'[10] It seems likely that eggs were offered because they are vessels out of which new life is born. The animal hatches from the egg, as the new month is born from the old; and the deity ensures the continuance of this process by which new life is handed on.

Another black Virgin who occupies a former Roman wayside is *Notre-Dame de la Mure*, near Cornas. The statue seems to be a copy of the Virgin of Le Puy, but she enjoys a cult of her own, and is reputed to have saved fishermen from drowning. Her shrine is close to the confluence of the rivers Rhone and Isère, which have both been important trading routes since ancient times.

Similarly, Our Lady of La Délivrande, near Douvres in Normandy, inhabits a crossroads which was formerly a site of Roman occupation. Above the chapel there rises a stream, which marks the boundary between the dioceses of Bayeux and Lisieux; so the Virgin is, as it were, the guardian of the boundary. She is also the protectress of sea-farers; and she grants fertility, as well as safe child-bearing. The name 'La Délivrande' is sometimes said to owe its derivation to the fact that the Virgin here delivers prisoners from captivity. Saillens, however, states that as recently as the 16th century, Notre-Dame de la Délivrande was called 'Notre-Dame de l'Yvrande'. The name *Yvrande* comes from a Celtic word meaning 'water boundary', and it therefore suggests that the stream where the shrine is situated may have been a territorial boundary from before the time when the Church imposed its diocesan organization upon the area.[11]

The transformation of the title 'de l'Yvrande' to 'de la Délivrande' is surely of considerable significance. It might be nothing more than an intelligent guess at the etymology of a name whose meaning had been forgotten. However, in the light of the traditions surrounding both La Délivrande and other shrines of black Virgins, it is reasonable to suggest that there is an intrinsic connection between the guarding of a boundary and the freeing of captives. For one of the most dramatic examples of transition from one place to another – from one side of a boundary to the other – is surely the passage of the released prisoner, who moves through the prison gate, from captivity to freedom. We have already seen that Mary guards the way that leads between Heaven and Earth, between below-ground and above-ground, and between lands which are separated by a sea voyage. But there are few boundaries more difficult to penetrate than those of the prison; and there are few transitions more deeply desired than the release of the prisoner who longs for freedom. Small wonder, then, that the Virgins who have authority over places of transition should also have the power to liberate captives.

The hymn *Ave Maris Stella*, sung at Orcival, includes a reference not only to the sea, but also to the freeing of those who are held in bondage. The third verse of the hymn runs as follows:

Solve vincla reis,	Break open the world's chains,
profer lumen caecis,	bring forth light for the blind,
mala nostra pelle,	drive away our evils,
bona cuncta posce.	plead for all good things.

Our Lady of Orcival is especially famed for setting captives free. Indeed, one of her titles is 'Our Lady of the Irons', because of the prisoners' irons which have been left at her basilica in thanksgiving for deliverance from bondage (Fig.4). Moreover, this Virgin's power to liberate has been experienced as recently as the 1940s.

During the Second World War, the people of Clermont-Ferrand rose up against the Nazis who had taken control of their city. Because of the insurrection, a very large number of men from the area were taken away to Germany as forced labour, and among them was the Bishop of Clermont, Gabriel Piguet, who is still remembered as an heroic opponent of the Nazi occupation. While the men were held in exile, they prayed to Our Lady of Orcival for their safe return. When this was eventually secured, after the Allies' victory, Bishop Piguet led the former captives in a pilgrimage of thanksgiving to the Virgin who had delivered them from their bondage.

For Christians, the imagery of captivity and freedom has

always been of great importance. This is partly because the early Church was persecuted and its members imprisoned. But it is also because Christians have experienced a dramatic sense of liberation when they accept God's forgiveness and begin to live a new life in Christ; it has often felt as though their old lives had been ones of slavery to sin, in contrast to the joyful privilege which they now experience as children of God (cf. John 8:34; Romans 8:15).

Sometimes people have carried out physical enactments of their bondage to sin and their liberation by Christ. At Rocamadour, for example, Henry II of England expiated the murder of Thomas Becket by kneeling in chains in the presence of his army, and praying for forgiveness. Likewise, ecclesiastical courts in Germany would send convicts to Rocamadour to do penance for their sins. The penitent would be bound in irons and chains until he had carried out the final rite of expiation, and would then be set free from his fetters.

When the Virgin's devotees have wanted to carry out a symbolic act of release for those in captivity, the gesture has sometimes consisted in the literal freeing of prisoners from jail. In Paris in the 16th century, a confraternity was formed under the patronage of Our Lady of Safe Deliverance, the Black Virgin of Paris. This was a voluntary organization of lay people, who conducted acts of worship and carried out works of charity. Their particular concern was the liberation of captives, and on their major festivals the confraterniy would hold an elaborate procession through the streets of Paris. At the end of the day, the confraternity would go to the debtors' jail with money which members had given, and with it, they would buy the release of as many prisoners as they were able to.

In the Gospels, when Jesus teaches his disciples the Lord's Prayer, he uses the words 'free us from our debts' (Matthew 6:12). We usually translate this as 'forgive us our trespasses', but in Greek – and, indeed, in the standard Latin translation – the words can carry the literal significance of cancellation of debts, as well as the metaphorical meaning of forgiveness of sins. The devotees of the Black Virgin of Paris were thus enacting a symbolic gesture of divine mercy, as well as carrying out a material act of compassion. In the *Ave Maris Stella*, the worshipper appeals to the Virgin both to 'break open the world's chains', and to 'drive away our evils': the one is parallel to the other.

To be unburdened of the obligation to pay a debt is an experience of immense liberation; and it is for this reason that the cancellation of debts provides a powerful image for the Christian experience of being released from bondage to sin. Moreover, it is this liberation from sin which provides the foretaste of eternal life, and thus offers an assurance that the transition from this life to the next can be accomplished in safety.

From Death to Life

The boundary between life and death often presents greater hazards and fears than any other place of passage, but the Virgin of Orcival is attributed with power over even this, the most inevitable of all points of transition.

Among the miracles of Orcival, recorded as recently as the 19th century, perhaps the most remarkable are those which describe the revival of still-born babies. People were concerned about the fate of an infant who died without having been christened, since they believed that without baptism, the child would not be received into Heaven. It was the custom of the people in the mountains around Orcival to bring these dead infants to the shrine and present them before the miraculous image of the Virgin; they would pray to her to bring the child back to life so that it could be baptized. The child would be revived for long enough to receive the sacrament, and would then die with the guarantee of salvation and eternal life.

Here is a translation of an inscription which was given to the shrine of Orcival in thanksgiving for the miraculous revival of a still-born infant:

A child, whose father is called François Dumont and whose mother is Anne Biète, of the village of Brousse, in the commune of Le Mas and canton of Auzances (Creuse), dead before birth and consequently deprived of the grace of baptism, was carried, at his mother's vigorous insistence, by his grandmother and his aunt, who arrived barefoot in the church and in front of the miraculous statue of Our Lady of Orcival, on the 30th October 1862, three days after the birth of the child. Suddenly, at the feet of Her whose every request is granted by Jesus, her divine Son, and in the wake of fervent prayers, the child's face, his skin and his flesh, which were all carbonised and seemed to be putrefying already, became fresh and rosy, charmingly beautiful, in the presence of a large number of people who were astonished and overjoyed at this marvel. This child, in a word, gave such obvious signs of life that he was baptized. The next day he was interred in the parish cemetry.

The priest who carried out the baptism, the abbé Mallet, confirmed in 1894 that he was still moved every time he spoke of this event; and he affirmed that the body had truly been decomposing and that the 'resurrection' was undeniable.[12]

This, and other similar accounts, present Our Lady of Orcival as having the power to enable a safe passage from this life to the next. She will even pull people back across the boundary between life and death, in order to ensure that they can be securely delivered to a joyful destination.

The accounts from the 19th century are, of course, couched in the language of Christianity. They are concerned with Christian rituals, and with a Christian concept of Heaven. However, there is reason to believe that the powers which govern the passage between life and death have been venerated at Orcival since long before the advent of Christianity to this region.

When Frances Gostling visited the shrine in the early years of the present century, she entered into conversation with the old woman who was giving out candles. Amongst other things, the old woman said to the visitor, 'Before the statue of Our Lady was brought here, they say that the people were heathens, and worshipped a god called Orcus'.[13] Orcus was the god of death, from whom we get the word *ogre*. He was a dog or wolf, who fed on the flesh of the dead. Saillens states that he was Hecate's dog. Hence, one might expect that people would appeal to the goddess to protect them from her ravening hound. Hecate herself carried a torch, or torches, with which she would light the way to Hades. She was guide on the journey to the Underworld. Her association with points of transition – such as crossroads, and the turning of the months – thus extended to encompass the last and greatest of all boundaries: that between this world and the next. It may therefore be that Our Lady of Orcival is heir to a very ancient tradition of guardianship over the passage between life and death. Certainly, archaeological excavations have revealed Gallo-Roman settlement in the valley of Orcival; and the many springs which rise there suggest that it is a place at which there would have been a meeting and opening between 'this' world and the 'other' world.

Saillens believes that funerary rites persisted at Orcival well into the modern period. He says that people would take their shrouds there, and he quotes a 17th century author who wrote, 'the number of these offerings was unbelievable'.[14] Saillens does not speculate about the meaning of this practice, but an educated guess might suggest that the shrouds were being blessed prior to burial, in the hope of securing for the deceased a swift passage through Purgatory. Another possibility is that the consecration of the shroud would facilitate the journey of the departed soul from this world to the next, thus preventing the soul from being trapped on Earth as a ghost. In either of these cases, the Virgin is plainly being attributed with power over the soul's passage between Earth and Heaven.

Here again, we can see that the Christian doctrine of the Incarnation shows that Mary is ideally suited to perform this task. For as Heaven came down to Earth in her womb, so she can lead the creatures of Earth to Heaven. It is within her that the two come together.

However, there is another possible interpretation for the placing of shrouds in the shrine at Orcival. Consider the following miracle-story, which was recorded in the 18th century:

Two men of Saint-Amant-la-Chaire, considered to be dead, were on the point of being buried. One of their friends, emboldened by a great sense of confidence, made a vow to take them to Orcival where he would make an offering of the shrouds which were intended for the two men, if God would call them back to life. This act of faith in divine generosity touched the heart of the Sovereign Master; the two men, whom people had believed to be dead, gave first of all a few signs of life, and soon, completely returned to health, they presented themselves at Orcival in conformity with their friend's promise.[15]

In this case, the shrouds signify recovery of health. They are like the crutches which are left when the lame have been healed, or the chains which are brought when the prisoner has been freed. The shroud is no longer needed, and it is brought to Our Lady of Orcival because it is she who has snatched the petitioner from the jaws of death.

There are a number of accounts which describe people on the point of death, or who appear to be already dead, being revived at the invocation of the Virgin of Orcival. The image of Resurrection is, of course, at the heart of the Christian spiritual tradition, and a miracle of this kind reverberates through the Christian imagination. Christ's own Resurrection from the dead is the experience upon which the Christian Church was founded, and Resurrection is also promised for the righteous at the Last Judgement. In the Gospel stories, Christ's own Resurrection is foreshadowed in the raising of Jairus's daughter (Luke 8:40–56) and the raising of Lazarus (John 11:1–44), whilst the general Resurrection of the dead is prefigured when people arise from their tombs at the time of the Crucifixion (Matthew 27:51–53). Therefore, a story in which someone who is believed to be dead returns to life – a miracle of the kind which is associated with Orcival – is a reminder and a consequence of the Resurrection of Jesus. These miracles also point to the Resurrection of the dead on the Last Day, at the end of time. They call to mind the Assumption of the Virgin Mary when, at the end of her earthly life, she fell asleep and was taken bodily to Heaven. In this connection it is worth noting that Orcival possesses a monument known as 'the Virgin's Tomb'.

Over the centuries, the escape from death has been pictured in a variety of ways. It may be that death is seen as an all-devouring animal who can be evaded or propitiated in order to secure an after-life. (In Christian iconography, Hell is often represented as a gaping pair of jaws, which the souls of the damned are being tossed into.) Or death may lead to some sort of prison, in which wretched souls are hoping for release. I have already observed that when souls do not successfully accomplish the journey to the world beyond, they may be condemned to spend an indefinite period in a disconsolate state of wandering upon Earth. This is understood to be a condition which is imposed upon unwilling subjects who want to be released from it.

In the magnificent legend of the Harrowing of Hell, the Underworld is portrayed as a gloomy place to which the souls of the departed have been confined ever since the sin of Adam. Death is the conqueror, and mortal humanity must eventually succumb to his rule. When Christ dies on the Cross, however, he in turn conquers Death, and at this moment he descends to the nether regions. He then bursts open the gates of Hell, where, starting with Adam and Eve, he takes the hands of the righteous and, lifting them out of their miserable condition, leads them to eternal life.

The release of earthly captives from their bondage can thus come to signify the deliverance of the dead to perpetual joy. This parallel is suggested in another of the Resurrection miracles of Our Lady of Orcival.

This story concerns an event which occurred in 1640. A lady named Françoise de la Vergne lay ill in bed for about nine months, suffering from a condition which affected the heart and the brain. Physicians, apothecaries and surgeons were all unable to help her, and eventually she became quite still and lost all power of speech. She remained without speaking for three whole days. The doctors came to see her, and were of the opinion that she would not live beyond midday. Preparations were therefore made for constructing a bier and burying the lady, and candle-wax was obtained for the funeral lights. While this was being done, no-one could detect any sign of life in the patient, and there were clear indications of death. Several of her relatives and close friends were present, bewailing the captivity in which they found themselves; but they knew that several people had had recourse to the favours and prayers of the Virgin in the church of Orcival, and had received incomparable graces in similar and other states of captivity. They therefore made a vow and an act of devotion to the Virgin, in the place where Madame de la Vergne was lying. They had her winding-sheet put on her in the form of a shroud, and, at the moment at which they made their vow, they felt the lady's pulse beating and saw a change in her face. Life returned to the woman who was believed to be dead, and about four or five hours later, the power of speech also came back to her. Her companions then explained to her the vow they had made in the Virgin's honour. So the lady acknowledged the power and favour of the Virgin, and thanked her for her protection. Madame de la Vergne believed that it was through the Virgin's merit and favour that she had recovered her life.[16]

The narrative does not state the precise content of the vow which was made, but the context makes it reasonable to assume that the shroud was to be offered before Our Lady of Orcival in thanksgiving for the patient's recovery. The statement that she lay without speaking for three days before the miracle was worked, suggests conformity to the Resurrection of Christ, which took place 'on the third day'. The abandonment of the shroud likewise has a resonance in the Gospels, for when Jesus arose from the dead, he left the grave-clothes behind him in the empty tomb.

So why should miracles of Resurrection be attributed to the Virgin, rather than directly to Christ?

Well, a motif that is submerged, but nonetheless present, in Françoise de la Vergne's miracle is that of childbirth: that is to say, of resurrection from the dead as analogous to birth from the womb. We are told that she was ill in bed for 'about nine months', which is the length of a pregnancy. Then, when the moment of 'death-or-deliverance' is reached, the patient's companions feel that they are in a state of *captivity*, and it is this which they seek to be rescued from. It is death, like an ogre, which holds them captive. But note that the emphasis is on the captivity of the *friends and relatives*, not that of the dying or deceased woman herself. This seems comparable to the condition of the mother in labour, who is hoping to be safely delivered of her child. In English, we speak of a woman's 'confinement'. In the French narrative of Françoise de la Vergne, the word used for the relatives who were present is *parents*, which also carries the narrower, English sense of the term. The sick woman's attendants are thus presented as parents and midwives: they are released from their captivity when their companion is reborn after her own nine-month confinement in the sick-bed.

In fact, Christian art and poetry frequently render Christ's Resurrection from the tomb in terms which make it analogous to his birth from Mary's womb. Indeed, it may be that the hope for rebirth after death depends upon having faith in a birth-giving mother; for who else could accomplish such a feat? Julia Kristeva has suggested that the reason why Christians portray Mary at the foot of the Cross is that this maternal image acts as a kind of assurance that Christ's death will indeed give way to new life.[17] It is certainly the case that, for centuries, Christian poets and theologians have compared Mary's suffering on Calvary to the pangs of childbirth. Artists, likewise, have made the dead Christ in his mother's arms look similar to the Madonna and Child, as though his death is a preparation for new birth.

Black Virgins frequently have authority over the grave, and this may have a particular connection with their power over fertility and the welfare of women in labour. We have already seen that one black Virgin is called 'Our Lady of the Eggs', and the egg is a symbol of new life both within the natural order and beyond death. Christians use Easter eggs as a sign of the tomb which Christ burst out of, as a chick breaks out of its shell. As new life comes forth, it breaches the boundaries formed by the wall of the egg and the stone of the tomb. The Virgin promises rebirth to those who cross the boundary between life and death. Correspondingly, the vessel in which this new life has been formed will be sacred to her – be it an egg, a grave, or a womb.

Several black Virgins have their shrines in former burial grounds. At Clermont-Ferrand, the statue known as *Notre-Dame de Bonne Mort* was found in the Cathedral crypt, where it had been placed in the last century to be guardian over the tombs of bishops. At Chartres, the bodies of several Christian martyrs were once thrown into the spring in the crypt. At Riom, near Clermont-Ferrand, there is a black Virgin housed in the church of Le Marthuret, which was once a Christian cemetery.

However, one has to be a little cautious when drawing conclusions from this sort of evidence, since relics and graves have traditionally been sacred objects in Christianity. Indeed, from earliest times, Christians celebrated the eucharist over the bodies of martyrs. The black Virgins' presence at burial sites might therefore indicate something about Christianity in general, but not about black Virgins in particular. Nevertheless, a number of these Virgins occupy sites which were already associated with the dead in pagan times. Saillens believes this to be true of Rocamadour, for example.

Close to Rocamadour there is a dry valley which is called 'The Lady's Combe'. The Lady was said to have established a 'palace' called the *Palay des Alys*, and she would traverse the contryside by night with her companions, the *Alyssantes*. Saillens contends that the Lady is associated with the alder tree which, by tradition, is associated with the rites of death. Saillens therefore concludes that the pagan deity who was once supreme in the Alzou valley was a goddess who was queen of the dead.[18] This would make some sense of the tradition which holds that Rocamdour was a place of human sacrifice in ancient times.

To be ruler of the Realm of Death, however, can be very different from offering the hope of new life. To be confined for ever within the Kingdom of Hades and Persephone presents a prospect devoid of any joy. To say that Mary is the Empress of Hell, however, is to assert something very different. For although Christian tradition holds that there are souls who have been consigned to Hell as a just punishment, it also maintains that the gates of the Underworld have been opened once and for all, so that Death cannot now prevail against the Son of God and his Mother. And according to tradition, if sinners cry out to Mary when they reach death's door, then even at this final boundary she will rescue them from Hell and will set them on course for resurrection to new life. Mary holds the most extensive possible authority over points of transition, for she can lead people through the bounds of Death itself.

*

Of all the beautiful places in which black Virgins have chosen to be honoured, the hamlet of Ronzières, in the Auvergne, must be one of the very loveliest. It is set on a hillside of green pasture, overlooking a plain beyond which there are mountains. Ronzières has a sacred spring, and was used as a burial place in prehistoric times. Just below the ancient cemetery is the Medieval Christian church which houses the black Virgin; it is a very holy place.

The Virgin is seated above a marble altar. Just above the altar and below the Virgin's feet, an inscription has been carved in the stone and the letters gilded. It says *Terror daimonum*: 'the terror of demons'.

Black Virgins are black because their power is terrifying. Yet in a certain sense, that is precisely why they are to be trusted. Our Lady of Ronzières keeps places of transition safe for crossing because she keeps at bay the forces of evil that might otherwise harm the pilgrim. By the same token, she keeps the powers of Hell away from the graveyard, and thereby promises new life to the dead who rest within the belly of the earth.

Notes

1. F. Marian McNeill, *The Silver Bough: A Four Volume Study of the National and Local Festivals of Scotland, Volume One: Scottish Folk-lore and Folk-belief* (Glasgow: William McLellan, 1957), pp. 75 and 175.
2. Dom Jacques de Bascher, *La Vierge Noire de Paris* (Paris: Téqui, 1979), p 23.
3. Frances M. Gostling, *Auvergne and its People* (London: Methuen, 1911), pp. 268–9.
4. E. Saillens, *Nos Vierges Noires: Leurs Origines* (Paris: Les Editions Universelles, 1945), pp. 152–3.
5. Gostling, *op cit*, p.80. The black Virgin in this account may perhaps be Notre-Dame de Neyrat. This statue was originally in a church at La Croix Neyrat, a tiny rural place within the parish of Montferrand. The church was destroyed at the French Revolution, in 1793, but the statue was saved by a family who subsequently gave it to the parish church. The city of Clermont-Ferrand has now expanded to incorporate La Croix Neyrat, and the suburb has its own modern parish church in which the Black Virgin has been re-instated.
   If the statue which Frances Gostling refers to was indeed Notre-Dame de Neyrat, then Mrs Gostling underestimated the devotion which was paid to this little Madonna at Montferrand. Canon C. Pourreyron, writing in the 1930s, wrote of Notre-Dame de Neyrat: 'It is this miraculous statue which is carried in the sollemn procession of the Nativity', i.e., the Nativity of the Virgin, which is the patronal festival of Montferrand parish (C. Pourreyron,

Le Culte de Notre-Dame au Diocèse de Clermont en Auvergne Nancy: Editions F. Bost, 1936, p.228).

6.   Gostling, *op cit*, p.272.
7.   Gregory of Nyssa, Homily on the Annunciation (PG 62: 765–766). Extract translated by Phil Jenkins, from Costante Berselli and Giorgio Gharib (eds), *In Praise of Mary: Hymns from the first millennium of the Eastern and Western churches* (Slough: St.Paul Publications, 1981), p.26.
8.   Monsieur Mallet, the parish priest of Orcival, wrote in 1894:

> At nightfall, two processions with torches leave the church, singing canticles, and whilst one group goes off in the direction of the hill which commands the town to the south-west, the other goes towards the chapel of the spring ... The hymn *Ave Maris Stella*, sung antiphonally by the two groups of pilgrims, answering one another from one hill to the other, produces a marvellous effect.

(Mallet, Curé-Doyen d'Orcival, *Histoire d'un Sanctuaire d'Auvergne: Notre-Dame d'Orcival* Lille-Paris: Societé de Saint-Augustin; Desclée, de Brouwer et Cie., 1894, pp. 20–1.)

There is no indication of how ancient this practice is.

9.   The original image is said to have been destroyed at the Revolution, and replaced in the 19th century by a bare wood statue, 40 cm in height. Ean Begg writes that the statue was reported to have disappeared in 1920, but that the parish priest of Noves said in 1984 that it could be seen in the chapel (*The Cult of the Black Virgin* London: Arkana, 1985, p.230).

However, Sophie Cassagnes-Brouquet has published an apparently recent photograph of Notre-Dame des Oeufs, with the indication that the statue is now in a private collection. She suggests that it might date from the 14th century. This raises the possibility that her photograph shows the image which was venerated before the Revolution, and not its replacement – in which case, the figure was evidently not destroyed. It still seems to have a certain amount of paint on it, which does not conform to Begg's description of 'bare wood'; but it is 40 cm in height (*Vierges Noires: Regard et Fascination* Rodez: Editions du Rouergue, 1990, p.152).

10.   Saillens, *op cit*, p.124.
11.   Saillens, *op cit*, pp.64 and 190–1.
12.   Mallet, *op cit*, p.144.
13.   Gostling, *op cit*, p.14.
14.   Saillens, *op cit*, p.138.
15.   Mallet, *op cit*, pp.122–3.
16.   Mallet, *op cit*, pp.137–8.
17.   Julia Kristeva, 'Stabat Mater' (trans. León S. Roudiez), in Toril Moi (ed.), *The Kristeva Reader* (Oxford: Basil Blackwell, 1986), pp. 160–186.
18.   Saillens, *op cit*, p.153.

PART V

Revealed in Liturgy

Icon of the Heavenly City: Towards an Understanding of the Gothic Cathedral

Michael Reardon

The Heavenly Jerusalem

There is little evidence to suggest that the first generations of Christians attached any special value to the places where they worshipped. St Paul taught that God did not dwell in temples made by man, but in the heart of the believer and, in any case, the threat of persecution would have made the establishment of formal places of worship a dangerous luxury. When the faith became the official religion of the Roman Empire, and adopted its civil administration, the secular basilica began to replace the synagogue or house as a place of worship, and there are signs that a more than spatial value was attached to these. You can feel this, I think, as Augustine writes about the basilicas of Rome that had fallen into the hands of pagans and barbarians, and his feeling for architecture as a manifestation of harmonic order would echo down the centuries.

When the Church took over the sites of pagan temples, the special attributes of the place would influence the perception of the new building, just as the saint to whom it was dedicated often acquired the attributes of the supplanted deity.

Justinian's dedication of his great church at Constantinople to the Holy Wisdom, and the comparison he made with the Temple of Solomon, marked a significant step in the establishment of an association between the building of the church and the Celestial City of Ezekiel, of which the Temple of Solomon was regarded as an earthly forerunner, and by the 8th century, Consecration Rites make the Temple the antecedent and 'type' of the new building. The process of hallowing of the surrounding walls and the importance which was attached to the axis and orientation of the building, however, were almost certainly inherited from the pagan world and may reflect the foundation of cities in Roman or Hellenistic times.

By the 11th century, a richly furnished sanctuary invokes comparison with the Heavenly City – which is represented in painting and sculpture as a contemporary church. Later on, the metaphor becomes reversed so that, instead of the Heavenly City being a metaphor for splendour, the need to invoke that image justifies a splendour in building. This did not convince Bernard of Clairvaux, who forcefully reminded his contemporaries that the Holy Spirit did not dwell in the richly furnished quire, but in the naked poor at the monastery gate. His views were to have a profound influence on the development of architecture, but little effect on the ambitions of church builders. Throughout the next four centuries, huge amounts of labour and great sums of money would be devoted to building images of the Heavenly City in glass and stone.

The Age of Cathedral Building

The scale of church building in the 12th and 13th centuries demonstrates a high level of technical expertise and organization on the part of their builders, and certainly could not have been achieved by a primitive or entirely agrarian society. The 12th century was a period of both intellectual fertility and technical development. Through contact with the Arabic civilizations of North Africa and Spain, the scholars of Europe assimilated the scientific and philosophical thought of the Ancient World and this resulted in major advances in theoretical physics, applied mathematics and optics. There is a renewed interest in the art and literature of Greece and Rome and in the theories of Vitruvius; Giraldus Cambriensis visits and describes the ruins of Roman cities and theatres. The English friar, Roger Bacon, propounds the possibility of machines that might enable man to travel under the sea or fly through the air, or even harness the power of steam. There were many schools of philosophical inquiry and, even though travel was slow and often dangerous, ideas spread rapidly through the organization and common language of the Church.

This was also a time of economic growth, in which the agricultural production of Northern Europe increased, partly as a result of improved methods of cultivation and partly due to climatic warming – evidenced by the northward advance of viti-culture. The Cistercians, who were already using water power for industry, are thought to have started the selective breeding of crops and animals. There was a thriving international trade in commodities of all sorts, and a highly developed and well orga-nized building industry in France and England.

The City and The Virgin

Many new cities were founded at this time, often by King or Bishop and, like New Sarum, generally on sites advantageous for trade and expansion rather than defence. They were laid out on a regular grid, perhaps derived from Roman towns or from the pre-cepts of Vitruvius. The spirit of the age is exemplified by the City with its towering cathedral and busy market rather than the remote monastery. Scholarship thrived mainly in the schools attached to cathedrals and in cities like Oxford and Paris, and students came from all over Europe to hear famous teachers debate the new premises of science and philosophy. They lived in inns and hostels, rather than monasteries, where ideas could be more freely exchanged – though always under the watchful eye of the Church.

The Cathedral constituted a virtually self-governing city within the city, with gates like any city, emblazoned with the achievements of its Ruler. The roofscape of many cathedrals, like Exeter and Lincoln, were ornamented with the symbolic ele-ments of defence even though they were not, in practical terms, defensible. Throughout the Middle Ages outward appearance was an essential component of power, whether temporal or spiritual and, since literacy was not widespread, visual symbols, like those of heraldry, played an important role. You had to know to whom the City belonged and it is therefore significant that, above the doors of practically every gothic cathedral, regardless of formal dedication, there was a sculptured representation of the Virgin Mary, and often the most prominent position above the West Door was reserved for the Coronation of the Virgin as Queen of the Heavenly City.

The cult of the Virgin Mary had grown enormously in

popularity at this time. Cistercian influence may have been significant in this as Bernard of Clairvaux was especially devoted to her and was depicted being miraculously fed by milk flowing from the breasts of her statue – an allegory of Divine Wisdom. In the influential *Speculum Beatae Mariae*, she is described not only as Queen of Heaven and of Angels but of Demons, over which she was thought to have dominion. She is also associated with Solomon and with the Temple, linking Old and New Testaments and identified with the Woman Crowned with Stars in Revelation. As Queen of the Church on earth and of the Heavenly City, her power and attributes were, for many medieval churchmen, little short of divine.

Although the Rosary prayers were not formalized until much later, many of her titles, such as 'The Perfect Rose, A Garden Enclosed, A Tower of Ivory', etc. were in common use by the 12th century. From the 13th century onwards, her office was recited daily and the Angelus rung, and in most cathedrals, whatever their formal dedication, the liturgy of her feast days was the most splendid of all. These images have the quality of 'concentricity', which has been since pagan Antiquity a symbol of both the Ideal City and the Cosmos: 'Figlia del Tuo Figlio, Queen of Heaven'.

Screen and Iconostasis

In an Orthodox Church, the rood screen marks the boundary between the material world of now and the invisible one of the Heavenly Host and the face of the screen, like the surface of a holy icon, is the meeting point of two realities. Until the Reformation, our parish churches had screens which performed a similar role. With their images of mediating saints, the Rood and Judgement above, they set forth the Divine Oeconomy of Man's Redemption.

The ritual associated with this sacred 'proscenium', the passing through the screen and the raising and lowering of the Lenten veil, constituted much of the drama of medieval religion, just as it does in the Orthodox Church today. One may say that an Orthodox church is closer in spirit to a parish church of the

Middle Ages than our buildings now – but of course, in the 12th century, the Great Schism was a relatively recent event.

The screen itself probably developed out of the triumphal arch or *Porta Coeli* which, in the Early Christian basilica, stood over the High Altar. As the Sanctuary became identified with the Heavenly City, and the exclusive territory of the ministers of the Altar, it was logical for this to be at the entrance to the space rather than within it. In the new position it absorbed the Pulpitum and Ambo, and hence became known as The Pulpitum. In cathedrals and monastic churches it divided the Quire, where the community sang the daily Offices, from the Nave, accessible to the laity. One or more altars generally stood in front and, if it carried the Rood, one of these would be dedicated to the Holy Cross. In some greater churches however, the Rood Screen was a separate structure in front of the Pulpitum.

From the late 12th century, the west fronts of cathedrals began to develop into giant iconographic screens, representing God's scheme of creation and the Oeconomy of Salvation. This development seems to have been initiated and generally reached its fullest development on those cathedrals served by secular canons. This is not entirely surprising since the monastic rule favours an inward looking approach to life and ministry. This may also have been reflected in liturgical patterns and account for some of the architectural differences between cathedrals like Worcester and Salisbury.

The development of a principal external iconstasis seems to imply that it is the whole building, rather than the Sanctuary alone, which represents the Heavenly Jerusalem. This view is supported by the liturgical use of these fronts as we will see later on. That parish churches did not develop in the same way suggests that these were differently perceived, and that the cathedral was not simply a big church with a bishop's throne, but something entirely different.

The image of the cathedral as the Celestial City is also found in manuscript illuminations, where Solomon's Temple is usually represented as a gothic cathedral (and, for that matter, the Heavenly Jerusalem as a walled contemporary city). You get the sense of this by standing on the roof of Milan or Exeter cathedrals today. Events from the life of Christ or the Virgin are also depicted as occurring within a great church and in present time. The significance of this will be clearer when we come to nature of the Medieval Image.

The Architecture of Harmony and Light

Most people will immediately recognize that a Gothic building is quite different from the Romanesque, yet most of the distinguishing features of the latter: great height, flying buttresses, ribbed vaults and even pointed arches, can be found in the former. Nor is the plan of the gothic cathedral much different, and both grew out of a tradition of masonry construction dating back to Roman times. Why then are they so different and how did this change come about?

As in so many things at that time, Bernard of Clairvaux was significant in this since he disapproved of lavish ornament in churches, and demanded a more austere style of building for the houses of his reformed 'Cistercian' rule. In consequence, the churches built for this order were without painting or ornament and relied for their beauty on the expression of structure and the use of harmonic proportions. This gave promise of a new unity of form and decoration very different from that of Romanesque churches, where the Divine Oeconomy was represented in paintings and sculptures, often scantily related to the structural form of the building.

Geometry has always been used by architects as a tool in design and by masons for setting out the work but, for Medieval theologians, numerical relationships had profound significance. This derived from the proportions of Solomon's Temple, from the works of Pythagoras and Augustine. The philosophers of the 12th century saw the universe as a harmonic structure, embodying certain mystical proportions that are also responsible for the stability of matter. Some thought that the whole of Creation could be expressed in terms of number relationships and that these were paradigms of God's creative process.

Since mathematicians of that time did not have algebra or calculus, they used geometry to express mathematical concepts.

Applied to architecture, this meant that a building based on the same geometry as the Cosmos itself would thereby mirror its nature. Furthermore, the proportional relationships which underlie the stability of matter would also ensure the stability of a building – a premise that was not always fulfilled in practice. The choice of proportions for a building was, therefore, primarily a philosophical issue. This was clearly demonstrated in the debate about the design of Milan Cathedral, which turned upon the theological implications of the proportions to be used rather than any practical considerations.

Whilst these principles applied to all art, they were most significantly expressed in music, which was thought to embody mathematical relationships in their purest form, unencumbered by gross matter; music was the most important sign and attribute of the Heavenly Jerusalem just as cacophony was of Hell. The rise of the Gothic cathedral is paralleled in the development of polyphony and this form of music was an essential part of the liturgy. However, the designers of buildings had a symbolic language that was denied to musicians – the use of light.

The use of light as a symbol of the Holy Spirit derives directly from the Gospel of St John, and the concept of light as the purest form of matter from a mystical philosophical treatise known as the *Corpus Areopagiticum*, attributed to Dionysius, a Neo-platonist philosopher of the 4th century. Translated into Latin by Johannes Scotus Erigina early in the 12th century, it inspired a school of metaphysics which had a profound influence on the Abbé Suger when he came to rebuild the eastern end of the church of St Denis, around 1130. This may have been because Medieval historians had confused Dionysius the philosopher with St Denis, patron of the royal house of France, whose burial place the abbey was.

Whether theory or practice came first, it is generally agreed that the essential qualities of Gothic architecture came together for the first time in the Abbé Suger's choir and ambulatory. The structure was clearly articulated and decorative elements are subordinate to the structural form; each part of the building is related to the others by geometrical proportions. But what strikes the beholder above all is the way in which light pervades and penetrates the structure. This interested the Abbé so much that he devoted much of the guide book he wrote for the church to the symbolic implications of its appearance. Essentially, the building was worthy, not because it pleased the eye, but because in its forms and proportions it reflected the order of the Cosmos, and because the light penetrating and dissolving the solid masonry was a symbol of the nature and action of the Holy Spirit.

Throughout the Gothic period, transparency of structure to light and the luminescence of surfaces achieved by the interplay of light and colour, were the most valued qualities in sacred architecture. The single feature which most perfectly expresses the Gothic spirit is not the soaring vault, but the rose window filled with painted glass.

It is unlikely that the masons, carpenters, painters and metal workers who actually built the cathedral, would have understood the philosophical ideas behind it. Their labours, unless informed by sound proportions, were sometimes used by preachers as an example of chaos. So how would they have perceived the building? Since they have, for the most part, left no record of their thoughts, we can only answer that question by putting the cathedral in the context of other images, those of the Virgin or the saints, and considering how those were understood by ordinary people as well as the 'literati'.

The Use and Perception of Images

The Christian culture has always had an ambivalent attitude to visual images and this is, perhaps, implicit in the different nature of the Judaic and Hellenic cultures from which it derives. At risk of grave simplification, Hellenistic culture, and particularly Neoplatonism, was friendly to images and, from the teaching of Aristotle, it placed a high value on the sense of sight. Judaic culture, on the other hand, mistrusted visual art, particularly if representational, and Jews were specifically forbidden to make images of God. A cult based on divinely inspired laws embodied in sacred tablets, whose practice largely involved oration and prayer, was unlikely to give as high a position to the sense of sight. They had seen how the love of physical beauty could seduce men away from the worship of the One and only God.

For the early Christians, three-dimensional images were too closely associated with pagan cults for comfort, and it was only when victory over them was secure that images were given a role in worship. By this time, the membership of the Church included many illiterate converts for whom images were a useful means of instruction. Even so, their role was defined in strictly paradigmatic terms and, for fear of the ignorant being led into idolatry, lifelike images were better avoided. To this extent, Gregory the Great conceded a limited role to images. By this time, the Aristotelian view of the primacy of sight had gained ground and was beginning to erode the supremacy of the 'word', and images began to assume a greater role, at least in popular worship, than perhaps Gregory intended. It was probably a growing concern that this was in danger of returning the Church to pagan practice, together with theological arguments (and no doubt political motives), that fired the dispute known as the 'Iconoclastic Controversy', and some of the arguments fielded in that dispute are relevant to our understanding of the Medieval Image.

The opponents of images claimed that representing God involved circumscribing Him who cannot be circumscribed and all such images were therefore false. The only valid image of Christ is Eucharist – and any other would be superfluous. They also believed that the sense of sight is the most open to corruption and therefore an unworthy channel for Divine Truth. They claimed, not without justification, that lifelike representations of the saints were being taken for reality by ignorant people and venerated as if they were the real thing. Virtually identical arguments would be put forward in the future by Cathars, Lollards, the followers of Luther and Calvin and even by Catholic bishops at the Council of Trent.

Supporters of images argued that, since God was circumscribed by human nature in Christ, He could be depicted in art without falsifying His nature. They tended to hold a Neoplatonist view of the relationship between forms and particulars, in which Particular Things are seen as reflections of invisible but existent Forms of whose reality they partake. This is immensely significant for the understanding of the image since, if the particular chair shares in the reality of the 'eternal chair', then an image of Our Lady can share in Her reality. This led to the concept of a hierarchy of forms, by which truth reaches our understanding, which was developed by John of Damascus into a vision of a Great Chain of Images though which the truth of God is revealed to Man. This suggests that the making of images is not only permitted to Christians, but is a necessary component of enlightenment and worship. Images are, like the Holy Church itself, a part and continuation of the Incarnation. Similar arguments to those put forward later, by Walter Hilton, against the Lollard iconoclasts. However, the Orthodox Church required that images must not be 'lifelike', whereas the Western Church did not.

For the Catholic West, the nature and use of images was defined by Thomas Aquinas, probably influenced by John of Damascus. Aquinas distinguishes carefully between the Image as a Particular Thing – that is a piece of stone or wood – and the Image as a 'mirror' of what it represents. Whilst no reverence is due to it in the former sense, the same reverence may be offered to it in the latter sense as would be given the person it represents. A sound distinction in philosophical terms, but one that meant little to the ignorant – as any Medieval bishop could have told him. This definition is however, essential to the understanding of all Medieval art – including the Gothic Cathedral.

The Theatricalization of the Image

As time passed the distinctions so carefully made by Aquinas between the particular object and the thing it represents became ever more blurred in the popular mind. This process has been related to the development of Eucharist theology. Although transubstantiation was not declared a doctrine of the Church until the 16th century, belief in it had been endorsed by the Lateran council of 1215 and popular credence in transubstantiation, often in an extreme form, was undoubtedly reinforced by the institution, in 1264, of the Feast of Corpus Christi – for which Aquinas wrote an Office. The notion that two natures or two levels of reality can subsist in the same object is obviously significant for the perception of images. Moreover, since transubstantiation is a consequence of the 'act' of consecration, it also has implications for the perception of reality in the theatre, and it may not be entirely coincidental that the feast of Corpus Christi became an occasion for the performance of cycles of religious plays, of which the most elaborate and splendid took place in cathedral cities.

When relatively few people can read, both mental concepts and personal experiences which, in a verbal culture would find their expression in words, are likely to be expressed in a more theatrical way, and when the subject transgresses the 'natural' order, these will appear as 'miracles'. For example, views of the nature of the consecrated host were expressed in events like the 'Miracle of Bolsena' or the 'Sangue Prodigioso' of Ferrara. Certainly, in the later Middle Ages, the distinction between image and reality seems to dissolve with increasing ease and frequency. Crucifixes speak, statues of the Virgin weep or lactate, and images step down from their niches to interfere in the world's affairs. Some of these events clearly express the need of the beholder for help or comfort in a mysterious and often threatening world. Others clearly had a didactic content, like the image of Virgin and Child at Coventry that made gestures to illustrate the Creed. No doubt credulity was exploited, but this alone will not explain all these events and nor was everyone who witnessed them ignorant or simple-minded. Such events were, for the beholder, 'real' and, in this context, can be accepted as such. But with what level of 'reality' are we dealing, and can this phenomenon be attributed entirely to the influence of a theological doctrine that relatively few people understood?

The great historian, Huizinga, thought that the increasingly lifelike quality of late Gothic sculpture was a major factor, but it can be argued this was another symptom rather than a cause. There were certainly other factors. The renewed interest in Classical sculpture, Automata and 'action statues' like the 'Vierge Ouvrante', may have been more common than we suppose. These would all have tended to blur the distinction between the animate and the inanimate. However, an extraordinary sense of 'life' – as if the distinction between the organic and the inorganic is dissolving before our eyes – is a quality in the carving of the 13th and early 14th centuries. It might even be described as an 'indwelling of the Spirit' in material things, to which Adrian Stokes' phrase 'The flowering of Stone', is as applicable as to any work of Quatrocento Italy.

The devotional use of images was undoubtedly influenced by the contemporary understanding of the process of perception, in which a physical 'ray', projected from the eye, was reflected back to the beholder and imprinted the image in the heart – which was regarded as the seat of personality. Since the image gazed upon partook of the essential nature of what it represented, a spiritual benefit derived from simply gazing upon 'good' images – such as those of Christ's Passion.

This was the rationale of 'Devout Beholding', which was so popular in the later Middle Ages. It is also the background to the visions of Julian of Norwich, of which J.T. Rhodes used the telling phrase, 'The invention of the devotional present'. I believe that they are of a piece with the 'theatricalization' of inner experience and with the present realism of late Medieval art, in which the Virgin and Christ-child are represented in a contemporary setting and in present time. Julian would, of course, have been familiar with devotional art of this sort and, before her enclosure, would probably have witnessed the Mystery and Miracle plays of her native city.

In plays, the three levels of creation were represented by levels of staging: Hell below, Heaven above and the present world in the middle. As in the plays, where angels and demons passed from one level to another, it was popularly believed that the inhabitants of the other worlds could enter this – demons to do mischief and angels to help and protect. For those in trouble, the forces of good were most accessible in certain places such as shrines containing the relics of a saint – whose 'real presence' was thereby guaranteed just as the consecrated host signified the presence of Christ. The Heavenly world was also accessible in cathedrals and great churches, which were held to reflect the Heavenly Jerusalem. This is charmingly illustrated by the smiling angels who ascend and descend the ladder to Heaven on the West

Front of Bath Abbey, recalling the vision of Jacob, 'Surely the Lord is in this place; and I knew it not . . . this is none other but the house of God, and this is the Gate of Heaven.'

The reality which the great cult images had come to possess by the end of the Middle Ages, is nowhere better demonstrated by the way in which many of them, like that of Walsingham, were imprisoned and executed during the Reformation as if they were real people – which indeed, to many, they were. The issues raised by the destruction of images undoubtedly resulted in a degree of 'culture shock' to which is difficult for us appreciate, and the issues were as much a perceptual thing as religious. This is evident from the excuse offered by a gentleman of Gloucester, in the reign of Elizabeth I, for his destruction of windows in the cathedral: 'These are not God'. ·

Although the two natures of the image, and the sense of two levels of reality that it engendered, deserted the Church, it survived on the stage where the 'real' power of the image appears again in Elizabeth's reaction to the performance of *Richard II* and the fears attached to performing Marlow's *Dr. Faustus* or the 'Scottish Play'. It survived too in the Tudor and Stuart concept of Kingship, and in the end, perhaps it was the destruction of the cult images of the Middle Ages that prepared the way for the death of a royal icon on the scaffold in Whitehall.

Iconography and Theatre

Writers on Medieval iconography seem often to ignore the impact of religious drama, of which there appears to have been a veritable explosion in the 12th century. Since the earlier spoken text was in Latin, the plays must have relied for their popular impact on lifelike staging – and there is considerable evidence that this was the case. Plays were often associated with cathedrals, and may sometimes have been performed in front of them using the West Front as a backdrop. The West Front of Lincoln has features, never fully explained by architectural historians, which may well be connected with this use.

Few stage directions of the period survive, but those that do, the Jeu'd'Adam for example, describe the costumes, scenes and gestures for the Judgement. The relative positions of Hell and Heaven are described. Heaven is an orderly place with musical instruments, trees and fruit. Hell is noisy and chaotic with demons and cauldrons of fire. This is a description of a typical Judgement tympanum. We cannot, of course, be certain which came first but the common inspiration is clearly the Apocalypse. It has been suggested that, in some cases, the actors' costumes for plays like that of Daniel from Beauvais, mimicked the painted sculpture of the cathedral – but this we can never know for certain.

Bearing in mind the liturgical use of the West Front on Palm Sunday, to which I shall refer later, one should not dismiss the resemblance of these facades to the *frons scaeni* of a Roman theatre as accidental. Some Medieval scholars were not unaware of such structures and read, if not acted, the plays of Plautus and Terrence. They also had access to Vitruvius.

The Cathedral Liturgy

The Ruskinian concept of 'truth to the material' in art or architecture has made it difficult for people of this century to accept what the interior of a gothic cathedral really looked like.

The concept certainly meant nothing to the medieval architect or carver, for whom stone was a surface to be painted. Prior to the Reformation and the scrapings of the 19th century, it is unlikely that any unpainted masonry would have been visible within a Medieval cathedral. In order to get an idea of how they appeared, you must go to the 'Santo' at Padova or the Sainte Chapelle in Paris, where the surface decoration of the columns, vaults and walls has survived or been restored. In the richest gothic choirs, the profusion of highly polished marble shafts and lavish use of pigment and metal leaf must have given the impression that the building was made of metal rather than stone. A luminous, glittering shrine for some precious relic – which indeed is what it was, since not only the saints but God himself was mysteriously present within its walls.

Understandably, architectural historians have tended to regard the cathedral as primarily an architectural image, and a static one at that. This would not be in character with the nature of the

Church whose role was to present the Oeconomy of Salvation *in ille tempore*. This involved a changing scene, as altarpieces were opened and closed, and rich stuffs or greenery hung up, and rushes spread for important occasions. Images were carried in procession. On the feast of Pentecost, a mechanical dove might 'fly' on a wire through the building. The betrayal of Christ, or the three Marys seeking the tomb, would have been acted out dramatically. In shrine churches, the lifting of the canopy to expose the relics would be attended by the ringing of bells. Cathedral bells rang at intervals throughout the day signifying the hours of the Holy City to the city outside, markers of sacred time. But what part did the liturgy play in creating the image of the Celestial City, and how did it relate to the building?

The liturgy of Medieval cathedrals is the subject of current research, but some indication of how it may have related to the building is seen in the common use of the West Fronts of cathedrals on Palm Sunday, for a dramatic representation of Christ's entry into Jerusalem. At Salisbury, Lichfield and Wells, and perhaps elsewhere, singing tubes are built into the masonry so that the voices of boys in the wall passages behind the masonry would apparently emanate from the carved angels of the front itself. Elsewhere, an external singing gallery served the same function, as at Exeter. The resemblance of the Gothic cathedral front to the *Frons scaeni* of a Roman theatre has already been noted and here it is performing a similar function. The derivation may indeed not be all that far fetched since William of Blois, John of Salisbury and Vincent of Beauvais all had some knowledge of the Roman stage, and the plays of Terrence and Plautus were read by educated laymen.

At Salisbury and Exeter, where feast day liturgies (particularly those associated with the Blessed Virgin) were very elaborate, involving processions around the entire building to sung chants and antiphons at certain points or 'stations', they would certainly have been accompanied by musicians. Exeter has five musicians' stations at high level, including the Pulpitum, galleries in the transepts, one mid-Nave and at the West end, and four of them are connected by high level wall passages. Does this indicate that the proliferation of carved angelic musicians in this period signified real musicians, and the West Front was not alone in being 'wired for sound'? Did then clerestory and triforium passages permit 'angelic' music to accompany the processions below? If this were so, it would be of a piece with other theatrical ceremonial, particularly royal ceremonial, of the period and suggest that musical practices which we associate with 16th-century Venice, may have a longer ancestry than previously thought.

The processional use of the building is also of a piece with the nature of Gothic architecture itself, which is clearly intended to be 'read' sequentially, rather than from a central or fixed view-point like a Renaissance building. There are parallels, too, with the music of the period.

Some cathedral ceremonial is more mysterious in its intentions – like the circular 'dance' which the canons of Autun performed over the maze on the Nave floor at Vespers on Easter day. According to contemporary accounts, this involved a golden ball which was passed between the central figure and each dancer in turn, to the accompaniment of the Easter Sequence. Perhaps this had a cosmic meaning not unrelated to the cosmic imagery of some cathedral pavements. Certainly, the life of a great cathedral was clearly never dull!

Much of the music of these ceremonies would have been poly-phonic since this was the time of the *Ars Nova* of Philip de Vitri, Adam de La Hale and Machaut, and the instruments which appear in the hands of angelic musicians are likely to have been used in the liturgy too.

Like the Medieval king, the cathedral depended for its reality and power, not simply on a static majesty of appearance, but on vivid theatrical ritual. Once the reality of that image was destroyed, its power, like that of the Church itself, dwindled away to a beautiful but empty shell, frequented by antiquarians and useful for concerts.

Summary

I have attempted in this, rather unscholarly paper, to put down some markers to an understanding of the Gothic cathedral.

The Gothic cathedral was not a 'place of worship' in the sense that we use that term, but a image of the Celestial City and a mirror of the Cosmos. It was therefore not only a container of icons, but was itself an icon. Like other images, such as a statue of the Virgin, it was of two natures, and shared in the reality of what it represented. As an image it functioned in theatrical as well as architectural terms – and some of its distinct features may be related to this.

At a time when cathedrals are too often regarded as monuments or concert halls, or adapted rather awkwardly for parish-style worship, it is important to remember that they were built to be Images of the Heavenly Jerusalem, Mirrors of Creation and Icons of the Divine Oeconomy. Our equivalent might be to call them 'Theme Parks of the Divine Oeconomy', and perhaps we should see them in that light.

Who is the Woman Clothed with the Sun?

Ian Boxall

And a great portent appeared in heaven, a woman clothed with
the sun, with the moon under her feet, and on her head a crown
of twelve stars; she was with child and she cried out in her pangs
of birth, in anguish for delivery (Rev. 12:1–2).[1]

The Virgin Mother Clothed with the Sun?

In the National Gallery in London there hangs a magnificent
portrait of the 'Immaculate Conception' by the Spanish artist
Diego Velázquez. It presents Mary as a young girl, standing in
solitary splendour, and dressed in all the paraphernalia of
Revelation 12: clothed with the sun, standing on the moon, the
twelve stars silhouetted around her head. She stands suspended,
as it were, between heaven and earth, far removed from the rest of
humanity. Velázquez's painting is just one famous example of a
prevalent tradition in 17th-century Spanish religious art, which
saw in the vision of the Woman clothed with the Sun from the
Apocalypse of John a potent image of Mary conceived without
original sin.

Similarly, the image of the Woman clothed with the Sun has
served as a evocative symbol of the Assumption of Mary in
Christian devotion and iconography. As a child, long before I
ever became excited by this fascinating book, my only conscious
memory of the Apocalypse was in the Mass for the Feast of the
Assumption, where Revelation's vision of this mysterious woman
is the reading set. Moreover, I was reminded of the Apocalypse
every time I went into the Lady Chapel in my parish church,
where the statue of Mary portrayed her standing on the moon
(though lacking the sun and the stars), and victoriously treading
underfoot the unfortunate serpent, thus linking the apocalyptic
vision with a particular exegesis of Genesis 3:15, according to
which Mary is the New Eve bruising Satan's head. Thinking back

to it now, this statue was almost certainly a representation of the Immaculate Conception, though I took it to be a representation of Our Lady assumed into heaven. This connection between the Assumption and the Woman clothed with the Sun had been made by the Medieval Scholastics, and noted by Pius XII at the solemn definition of the dogma of the Assumption in 1950.

And yet one might legitimately ask whether, in the overtly mariological interpretation of the Woman clothed with the Sun, reflected in the liturgical and devotional celebrations of the Immaculate Conception and Assumption, Catholic Christians have not moved too far from the mind of John of Patmos? The problem is set in starkest relief when we look at the way in which the vision of the Woman was interpreted in the early centuries of the Church. For when we turn to the writings of the Fathers and surviving patristic commentaries on Revelation, we discover that the question as to the identity of the Woman clothed with the Sun appears to have found a rather different answer. I propose to review briefly some early interpretations of the passage about the Woman, before moving on to the vision itself to offer some thoughts as to an appropriate interpretation; and finally, I hope to offer some reflections on the devotional use of this image with respect to Mary.

Revelation 12 in Patristic Exegesis

To state the problem in all its starkness: the interpretation of the vision of the Woman clothed with the Sun as Mary, the Mother of the Messiah, appears to have been neither the most obvious nor the most widespread conclusion drawn by commentators on the Apocalypse in the first few centuries of the Church's life.[2] Though we must be cautious, given the relative paucity of the evidence we possess,[3] nevertheless the dominant understanding seems to have been that this woman represents not an individual, not Mary, but is a collective symbol for the Church, or the People of God of both Old and New Testaments.

Typical of this line of interpretation is Hippolytus of Rome in the early 3rd century. For Hippolytus, the whole vision concerns the persecution of the Church by the Antichrist, represented here by the great red dragon. The Woman clothed with the Sun, he claims, is the Church clothed with the Logos; her crown of twelve stars represents the twelve apostles by whom the Church is founded (*De Antichristo* 61).[4] And so we have a potent image of the Church, under persecution, giving birth to Christ in every age.[5] It was this line of interpretation – the Woman as a symbol of the Church, or God's faithful people in Israel and beyond – which the majority of commentators in the first six or seven centuries seem to have taken up and developed allegorically, often in rather fanciful ways. The Sun, for example, is understood by various patristic writers to symbolize either Christ, or the hope of resurrection; the Moon is understood variously as baptism, or the church of the heretics, or even John the Baptist; the attempt of the Dragon to destroy the child and the subsequent flight of the Woman into the wilderness represent Herod's slaughter of the innocents and the flight into Egypt.

Particularly interesting are those who see in the Woman a symbol not simply of the church, but of the People of God throughout history, acutely aware that, from an historical perspective, it was out of Israel that the Messiah was born. This line of interpretation is associated with some of the greatest commentators of the patristic period, such as Jerome, that great patron of biblical scholars, or Augustine, who saw in the Woman a vision of the 'City of God', or Victorinus of Pettau, who wrote the first Latin commentary on the book, and identified the Woman as 'the ancient church of the fathers and prophets and holy apostles'.

There were, however, those during this period, probably a minority, who made the identification between the Woman and Our Lady. Methodius, who died in 312, arguably knows of some when he comments on this passage; though he is quite scathing about them,[6] and is clear in his own mind that the Woman represents the Church, in her various aspects as Jerusalem, Mount Sion and God's Tabernacle. Several centuries later, Andreas of Caesarea, whose commentary on the Apocalypse became immensely influential in the Eastern Church, confirms that, by the time of Methodius, i.e. before 312, 'some' had already interpreted the Woman clothed with the Sun to be 'the all-holy Mother of God' (*In Apoc.* 33). And from later in the 4th century, St Epiphanius, Bishop of Salamis in Cyprus, notes the possibility that Revelation 12 may refer to Mary in his discussion of the disputed question of whether or not the Mother of God actually died (*Panarion* 78, 11, 3–4). Likewise, in the West in the 5th century, Quodvultdeus (d. 455), a friend of Augustine of Hippo, shows a tendency to supplement the dominant under-standing of the Woman as the Church with an recognition of Mary as the figure of the Church.

But it is not until the 6th century that we have an explicit and exclusive identification of the Woman with Our Lady preserved, in the first known Greek commentary on the Apocalypse, that of Oecumenius. Unfortunately for Oecumenius, however, given the growing tradition that Mary was exempt from the normal pains of childbirth, there is a difficulty with explaining the birthpangs, and not all will find his exegesis particularly convincing:

> Is there some contradiction? Not at all. The crying out in pain and distress is to be understood thus: Until the angel of God told Joseph concerning her, namely, that she had conceived of the Holy Spirit, she was in great sufferings, blushing most likely before her spouse and wondering if he suspected her to be pregnant from some secret marriage.[7]

The patristic evidence, then, is rather complex But, at least until Oecumenius, even those who held to a mariological interpreta-tion did not rule out the more widespread collective understand-ing, which continued to flourish, and later commentators held that the Woman was a symbol both of Mary and the Church. Might this be a possible way forward? In the light of this discus-sion I want to return to the primary evidence, Revelation 12, and suggest a possible reading.

Beginning to Understand the Apocalypse

Who, then, is this Woman clothed with the Sun, whom John sees in his vision on the island of Patmos? I want to begin by posing the more limited question which contemporary New Testament scholars have attempted to answer: who would the first hearers of the Apocalypse have understood this woman to be? That is an important question, and a crucial starting-point; but before we attempt to answer it, let us be clear that this is not the only legitimate question to ask. It is far from clear that the meaning of any scriptural passage can be exhausted by what its first hearers would have grasped, still less by what its author consciously intended, as the dominant historical – critical method has often assumed. This is not the way that Christian exegetes have approached scripture for much of the Church's life, nor, as I shall maintain below, is it particularly appropriate for understanding writings such as the Apocalypse whose images are so archetypal and fluid. Nevertheless, at least the primary historical meaning ought to exercise some control over the other meanings given to this passage. However, in order to tackle this question, we need first of all to set the vision in some kind of context. I want to suggest three things to bear in mind as we approach the Apocalypse.

First, biblical scholarship has in recent years learned, or rather relearned, to take seriously that this kind of book is precisely what it claims to be: an 'apocalypse', a 'revelation', an 'unveiling' of those things which human beings cannot otherwise see for themselves, because they are hidden from our limited view, beyond our limited perspective.[8] In short, the Apocalypse of John 'reveals' the true state of affairs as only God can see it, or, as Christ says to John in the opening vision of this book: 'Now write what you see, what is and what is to take place hereafter' (Rev. 1:19). The trouble is that many of us, including many within the Church, are handicapped by the popular perception of apocalyptic literature as primarily eschatological, to do with the 'End of the World', the destruction of the world as we know it. Our perception is formed by films with titles such as *Apocalypse Now*, by journalistic slogans about 'apocalyptic scenarios' which link the language of apocalypse to war zones and natural disasters, and by the fanaticism of religious sects such as the Branch Davidians of Waco, Texas, so much so that we find it virtually impossible to grasp that the book of Revelation is as much an 'unveiling' of 'what is' now as it is of 'what must take place hereafter'. But that is precisely what the book claims to do: to see it as exclusively, or even primarily about the End is surely to miss the point. What Revelation sees taking place in heaven is a kind of running commentary on what is happening, or will soon happen, on earth. Thus, when the Woman and the Dragon are seen, as great signs, in heaven, and the Dragon seeks to devour her newborn child, we can expect the same struggle to be taking place on earth, and not simply in the future, if only we can identify the Woman and her children.

Secondly, given that this is the case, New Testament scholars have come to recognize that the book of Revelation must have spoken in a particular way to John's contemporaries, living in the cities of Western Asia Minor in the second half of the 1st century. The trouble with so many popular and contemporary millenarian readings is that they treat the Apocalypse as if it were no more than a collection of predictions about the distant future, something like the Prophecies of Nostradamus, rather than having a message for the churches of John's own day. But the general consensus of scholars is that many of the allusions in the Apocalypse would have been readily intelligible to Christians living in the late 1st century. They would almost certainly have seen in the Harlot seated on the Beast, the opulence and corruption of the Roman Empire, not to mention the flourishing cult of the goddess Roma; they would probably have been able to correlate the heads of the Beast with recent Roman emperors, and even to 'reckon the number of the beast' (Rev. 13:18); they may well have understood allusions to past persecution and present difficulties being experienced by the churches (even if, as recent scholars have argued, the extent of actual persecution underlying the book has been vastly overstated).[9] Some of them may well have been shocked by the identifications that John makes between Satan and political, economic and religious systems, particularly if they are themselves implicated in them, but they would have been readily intelligible to them. Moreover, they would have been in a good position to identify the earthly counterpart of the Woman clothed with the Sun, and those of her children, within their own time.

Thirdly, however, this recognition that John was addressing

his contemporaries in a very direct way, while important for understanding what is going on and exercising some control on other readings of the book, cannot exhaust the meaning of the Apocalypse, which claims to describe visionary experience, albeit in narrative form. Apocalyptic symbols, as many commentators have pointed out, are evocative and polyvalent; their meaning cannot be exhausted by a single historical referent, and their greatest impact is made by their total effect. To try and translate them simply into propositional language robs them of their power. Just think for a moment of some of the images enshrined in the book: one cannot in any literal sense wash clothes white in blood, for example, and if one tries to visualize at once every aspect of the Beast from the earth, or the initial vision of Christ complete with sword issuing from his mouth, one very soon runs into difficulties, as the diversity of artistic representations of these visions will testify. Moreover, even those symbols which can be connected with historical events and personages, cannot be exhausted by them. Babylon may well be incarnated at a particular time in the Roman Empire, but Rome cannot exhaust the meaning of that image: the arrogant city can continue to be found throughout history, at every time and in every age, and indeed Christian commentators ever since have attempted to identify her in their own time. With these provisos in view, let us turn again to the Apocalypse.

The 'Four Women' of the Apocalypse

The human imagination has long been fired by the rather chilling vision of the Four Horsemen of the Apocalypse, an image which recurs again and again in Christian iconography and beyond. There are, however, also four women figures who feature prominently in the Apocalypse: three in the visions and one in the letters at the beginning of the book (Rev. 2–3). Of the three, the first is, of course, the Woman clothed with the Sun; contrasted with her is the Great Harlot, 'Babylon the Great, mother of harlots and of earth's abominations' (Rev. 17:5), who is seated on the beast; finally, and in even more striking contrast with Babylon, is the Bride of the Lamb, the New Jerusalem, who comes down from God out of heaven (Rev. 21:9–22:5). There is an interesting, if unexpected, relationship between these first three, which may shed some light on the identity of the woman who is our immediate concern.

Let us begin with the figure of the Great Harlot. It would not be difficult for the first hearers of the Apocalypse to recognize in her traits of the great Empire of which they were part. First of all, her mysterious name is 'Babylon the Great': any Jew would remember the Babylonian Empire as the destroyer of Jerusalem and its Temple, and it may well be that, by the time John was writing, the destruction of the Holy City, this time by the Roman Empire, was once again at the forefront of people's minds and exercising their theological muscles. Secondly, as if to confirm this, she is seated on the seven heads of the beast, which, we are told, are seven hills. The identification with the city of Rome could not be clearer. Yet that is not to say all that can be said about this woman. Rome is apparently only her present incarnation: she is not Rome, but the immoral, exploitative, oppressive city who can manifest herself in any age. But perhaps the most shocking thing about her is that she is a good deceiver, like the beast on which she sits: so impressive and seductive is this prostitute, that it is only through a divine revelation, through an apocalypse such as this, that she is shown up in her true colours, on the side of evil. To the naked eye, there is a very fine line between good and evil: even John 'marveled greatly' on seeing her (17:6), and it becomes clear that even some members of the Church have been taken in by her:

Come out of her, my people, lest you take part in her sins, lest you share in her plagues (18:4).

Contrast this woman, seated on the beast, who has seduced many, with the Woman clothed with the Sun, who is the enemy of the Dragon. If the Harlot is Babylon, the oppressive and self-indulgent city, then who is the Woman clothed with the Sun? When one reads, or better hears John's vision (for the Apocalypse was written to be read aloud), a kaleidoscope of images converge, merging together, forming new patterns, which makes it very difficult and indeed undesirable, to try and pin them down too precisely. We cannot rule out the distinct possibility that the first hearers of the Apocalypse would have seen in this vision echoes of Artemis, the moon-goddess of the local city of Ephesus; or the popular Eastern goddess Isis, whose cult had by this stage reached as far as Pompeii and Rome, and who was often portrayed in celestial clothing; or the story of the birth of Apollo, brother of Artemis, on the island of Delos, not many miles from Patmos, where his mother Leto had fled to escape the dragon Python, intent on destroying her divine child. Yet any pagan or mythological undertones have been heavily Christianized, and the images are primarily biblical.

To those who knew Israel's scriptures (and given the multiplicity of biblical allusions throughout the book, the author of Revelation assumed his readership would), this woman, adorned with sun, moon and stars, would echo the biblical image of Israel, God's Bride, who according to the Song of Songs is 'fair as the moon, bright as the sun, terrible as an army with banners' (Sg. of Sgs. 6:10). Her crown of twelve stars evokes the dream of the patriarch Joseph, who saw in the twelve stars himself and his brothers, the antecedents of the twelve tribes of Israel (Gen. 37:9–11). She is heavily pregnant, crying out in labour, like Jerusalem, who is portrayed by Isaiah as a pregnant mother, waiting to be delivered from suffering (Isa. 26:17–18a), and from the dragon Leviathan (Isa. 27:1); again like Jerusalem she is destined to become the mother of many children (Isa. 66:7–9). She gives birth to a male child, who is to rule or shepherd the nations with an iron sceptre, that is, the Messiah (Ps. 2:9). She escapes from the Dragon into the wilderness, being given eagle's wings to rescue her, like Israel, who at the Exodus was borne 'on eagle's wings' (Exod. 19:4) to escape the clutches of Pharaoh, and brought to a place of safety in the wilderness. And finally, we are told that the Dragon is defeated by the blood of the Lamb, that is, by her child, and that, in a furious rage, he pursues the other offspring of the woman, thus calling to mind the prophecy made to the serpent concerning Eve:

I will put enmity between you and the woman, and between
your seed and her seed; he shall bruise your head, and you shall
bruise his heel (Gen. 3:15).

To put it simply: the Woman clothed with the Sun is the heavenly counterpart of the messianic community, the People of God
(and John makes no sharp distinction here between historic Israel
and the Christian Church). She is the community which,
throughout history, has struggled to be faithful to God, not without trial and persecution, and out of whom was to come the
Messiah who would destroy the power of the Dragon.

Moreover, the birth of her child, amid birthpangs and great
torment, does not refer to the incarnation, to the birth of Jesus at
Bethlehem: as some of the earliest patristic commentators noted,
Christ was not immediately 'caught up to God' as a baby. Rather
it refers to his death and resurrection,[10] which resulted in the
exaltation of Christ to God's throne and the birth of a renewed
community. Revelation has already spoken of Christ as the
'firstborn from the dead' (Rev. 1:5; cf. Col. 1:18), and now, in a
heavenly vision, we see him being born into resurrection life.
There is an interesting parallel to this in the Gospel of John,
which describes the community's anguish in witnessing Christ's
death and resurrection in terms of birthpangs:

> Truly, truly I say to you, you will weep and lament, but the
> world will rejoice, you will be sorrowful, but your sorrow will
> turn into joy. When a woman is in travail she has sorrow,
> because her hour has come; but when she is delivered of the
> child, she no longer remembers the anguish, for joy that a
> child is born into the world. So you have sorrow now, but I
> will see you again and your hearts will rejoice, and no one will
> take your joy from you (Jn. 16:20–22).[11]

Finally, the Woman has a place prepared for her by God in the
wilderness, for the biblical 'a time, and times, and half a time',
that is for a limited period (cf. Dan. 12:7). But where is this place
which has been prepared for her? And what is to happen after this
'one thousand two hundred and fifty days'? Is this the last time

she appears in the Apocalypse? Surely this cannot be the end of the story for the Woman, for when we leave her, she is still threatened by the Dragon, as are her children.

Might it not be that this Woman appears again towards the end of the book, though in a rather different guise? This brings us to the third woman, the Bride of the Lamb, the New Jerusalem. She appears coming down out of heaven from God, having been prepared for her husband. She has now laid aside her celestial clothing, the sun, moon and stars, and is dressed instead in 'fine linen, bright and pure' (Rev. 19:8), which are the righteous deeds of her children. In other words, she has only now come to be what she was called to be through the faithful witness of her children throughout history (cf. 12:17). Now that Babylon the Great has fallen, and is no longer able to seduce the Church (Rev. 17), and now that the Dragon and the beasts have been destroyed and are now longer able to threaten God's faithful people (Rev. 20), the Woman is ready for her husband. The fluidity of apocalyptic symbols, unintelligible if taken literally, can allow the Mother of the Messiah, the community out of which he comes, now to become his Bride. Again, the Prophet Isaiah sheds light on the vision, in an oracle speaking about the vindication of Jerusalem:

> For as a young man marries a virgin,
> so shall your sons marry you,
> and as the bridegroom rejoices over the bride,
> so shall your God rejoice over you (Isa. 62:5).

But I said there were four women in the Apocalypse. There is one more, referred to in the letter to the church at Thyatira in chapter two. She is apparently a Christian prophet, a prominent member of the Church; thus she should be one of the children of the Woman clothed with the Sun; and that is no doubt what she believes herself to be. Yet John gives her the name of the pagan queen, Jezebel, and speaks of her in terms reminiscent of the Great Harlot, Babylon: she is criticized because she is too heavily implicated, perhaps unwittingly, in the idolatrous, immoral city, and encouraging fellow Christians to do the same in the name of

Christ. 'Jezebel' in the Thyatiran church is a salutary reminder that the Church, and prominent members of it, can be as much like the Harlot as she can be like the Woman clothed with the Sun. Christians in every age have not been immune to the lures of power or success, or to compromise and silence which allow the innocent to suffer. The Woman clothed with the Sun, whose children keep the commandments of God and bear the testimony of Jesus, has yet to become the Bride of the Lamb, the Heavenly Jerusalem.

Mary Clothed with the Sun in Christian Devotion

Given this interpretation of the women in the Apocalypse, is there any place left for Our Lady? I would suggest that there is, so long as use of Revelation 12 in Marian devotion attends to the primary reading of this passage that I have outlined above. However corporate the woman image, nevertheless her child is the Messiah, who is distinguished in the vision from the 'rest of her children' (v. 17). Is it not legitimate, then, indeed, is it not highly appropriate, to see in the figure of the Woman clothed with the Sun not simply her historical realization in Israel or Zion, but also, and especially, Mary, that member of God's People who became in history the mother of the Messiah? We cannot know for sure whether John had her consciously in mind in describing this vision, or his readers in hearing it: it is impossible to rule that out as a possibility. But in any case, given the fluidity of apocalyptic images, the meaning of the image is not exhausted by the conscious intention of the author, and the Marian interpretation need not undermine but can, rather, support the collective interpretation offered above. Moreover, when one locates the book of Revelation in the New Testament canon, alongside Luke who portrays Mary as the faithful Daughter of Zion (Lk. 1), and the Fourth Gospel, where she stands as the model of the Church at the foot of the cross (Jn. 19), waiting like a woman in travail (cf. Jn. 16:21) to see her son born into eternal life, the secondary Marian interpretation becomes even clearer. Nevertheless, the primary reading of this passage exercises some control over what we can say about Mary as the Woman clothed with the Sun: the interpretation of the vision offered here allows us to see the Woman not as Mary only, but Mary in that she represents, or sums up what it means to be the People of God, the model as it were for God's faithful people. What might all this mean for Marian devotion?

First of all, Mary, as the Woman clothed with the Sun, does not, cannot stand alone. One of the dangers of a particular form of Mariology, and indeed a particular presentation of the Marian dogmas of the Immaculate Conception and Assumption, is that it tends to isolate Mary from the rest of humanity. By stressing her privileges and unique status, rather than her particular vocation within and as one of God's People, there is a distinct danger of losing sight of the biblical origins of Mariology. It is a tendency which arguably is there in Velázquez's portrayal of the Immaculate Conception, a lone figure suspended between heaven and earth, and it is a danger in recent calls for Our Lady to be solemnly declared 'Co-Redemptrix' and 'Mediatrix of all graces'. But it is not an inevitable tendency of Mariology; and surely one of the insights of the Apocalypse is that Mary cannot be separated from God's people, but is rather the 'jewel' in its crown. Is it not possible to see in the Immaculate Conception of Mary the victory of divine grace and thereby an assurance of our own redemption; or to see the Assumption as the celebration of our own destiny, to share as embodied human beings in the vision of God? It was surely the Spirit at work among the Fathers of the Second Vatican Council which prompted them to locate their theological reflection on Mary at the heart of the Dogmatic Constitution on the Church, *Lumen Gentium*.

Moreover, the fact that the Apocalypse makes no sharp distinction between the People of Israel and the followers of Jesus in the vision of the Woman surely prompts reflection on the place of the Jewish people in God's plan of salvation. If Mary cannot be separated from the Church as her offspring, then neither can this Jewish mother of the Messiah so readily be divorced from the nation which nurtured her and prepared her for her vocation, and of which she is the supreme representative.

Secondly, there is surely significance in the fact that the 'birth' of the male child is no mere reference to the historical birth at

Bethlehem, but rather to the cross and resurrection, which issued in the birth of a new people. One of the insights of patristic exegesis on this passage is that the birth of Christ is not something to be confined to past history, but that the Woman as the Church is called to give birth to Christ in every age. If that is the case, then Mary can be celebrated in this vision not primarily as the one who bore him in her womb, but as the archetypal disciple, or even the foremost midwife, nurturing new disciples and enabling them to grow into Christ. This reminds us, moreover, of the goal of all devotion to and reflection on the role of Mary: to lead us to her Son. In this context those evocative words of St Paul, so reminiscent of the vision of Revelation 12, come to mind: 'My little children, with whom I am in travail until Christ be formed in you . . .' (Gal. 4:19).

Thirdly, in our concentration with the Woman, we should not overlook the battle with the Dragon, which is an integral part of this vision. There is a second painting by Velázquez in the National Gallery, entitled 'St John the Evangelist on the Island of Patmos', which many art critics regard as forming a pair with his 'Immaculate Conception', and which brings this theme to the fore. It presents the seer seated as if in contemplation, quill in hand and ready to write; in the top left hand corner, we see the Woman, this time with her protective eagle's wings, standing alongside the serpent-like Dragon with his seven heads, poised as if for the kill. The battle on earth between the Woman and the Dragon, paralleled by the heavenly battle between Satan and the archangel Michael, is an ongoing battle in which all the Woman's offspring are called to be involved. Interestingly, at a time when many in the Northern Hemisphere have largely dismissed the Apocalypse as the preserve of students of antiquity or religious cranks, Christian base communities in Latin America have found in the vision of the Woman and the Dragon inspiration for their ongoing struggle against injustice. For such Christians, Our Lady is their source of hope, the one who has already overcome the Dragon, and the one with whom they will battle against the particular manifestations of the Dragon in their specific socio-political situation. Whatever one's view of liberationist exegesis, and whatever one makes of the specific attempts to 'unmask' the

Dragon (Cuba and Nicaragua are sometimes mentioned as countries which have managed to expel the Dragon from their midst), 'God's little people' of Latin America have surely seen in the apocalyptic vision something to which many others have become blind: the centrality of the biblical doctrine of justice, which declares that injustice in all its forms has had its day; the extent to which, in every age, the Dragon can be found incarnated in political, religious and socio-economic institutions (cf. Rev. 13); finally, the call to all the children of the Woman to join with her through faithful witness in this ongoing battle. Neither is this a simple battle between insiders and outsiders. The shocking message of the letter to Thyatira, and of the vision of Babylon the Great, is that Christians can belong to the Harlot just as much as they can to the Woman clothed with the Sun. If Mary is the champion of justice, then she is such even within the Church, and the veneration of Mary as the Woman clothed with the Sun, the Mother of God's embattled people, should represent a necessary antidote and challenge to injustice wherever it may be found.

I want to finish with another example from Latin America, this time from Mexico, in which many of these aspects of the Woman clothed with the Sun come together in the person of Mary: the apparitions of Our Lady of Guadalupe to the Mexican Indian Juan Diego. It is securely significant that, when the Virgin appeared to this Indian in December 1531, in the early years of the colonization of Latin America by the Spanish, she appeared in terms reminiscent of the Woman of Revelation 12. The image which, it is claimed, was miraculously imprinted on Diego's cloak, and which may still be seen in Guadalupe today, presents Mary clothed with the sun, standing on the moon, her mantle decorated with the stars. According to the earliest transcript of the apparitions (written down within two years of the events), the woman asked for a church to be built on the site, with the promise that here:

> . . . I will show my loving favour and the compassion for the natives and for those who love and seek me, and for those who will seek my protection and call on me in their labors and

afflictions; and where I will hear your weeping and prayers to give you consolation and relief . . .'[12]

The precise significance of these events, religiously and politically, is of course complex, and the ways in which the devotion was received and used manifold: the location of the apparitions, for example, on the site of a former pagan temple can be read either as as sign of the resounding victory of Christianity over Aztec religion, or as a divine recognition of the spiritual aspirations of the indigenous people. However, one possible reading of the whole phenomenon, and one taken up by at least some compatriots of the seer, has found profound significance in the identification of the Virgin Mother, hitherto associated with the conquering Spaniards, with the local Indians, even to the extent of addressing Juan Diego in his own language, not the language of the colonizing people. Later popular devotion came to speak of her as the 'Dark-skinned Mother of Heaven', seeing in her features the features of the indigenous people, and she is now honoured as the patroness of Latin America. Is it not appropriate that at that time and in that place, Mary is seen and honoured as the Woman clothed with the Sun, the representative and personification of the faithful and, at times, persecuted people of God, God's vulnerable people who have conquered the Dragon 'by the blood of the Lamb and by the word of their testimony' (Rev. 12:11)?

Notes

1. Biblical quotations are taken from the *Revised Standard Version*.
2. For the relevant texts and discussion, see B. Le Frois, *The Woman Clothed with the Sun (Ap 12), Individual or Collective?* (Rome: Orbis Catholicus, 1954), ch. 1. For a full discussion of the history of interpretation of this vision up to the 20th century, see Pierre Prigent, *Apocalypse 12: Histoire de l'exégèse (Beiträge zur Geschichte der biblischen Exegese 2*; Tübingen: JCB Mohr (Paul Siebeck), 1959).
3. The earliest surviving commentary, that of Victorinus of Pettau, is from the late 3rd or possibly early 4th century, and we often have to rely on throwaway remarks from various Fathers writing on diverse subjects.
4. Le Frois, pp. 49–50, suggests that Hippolytus implicitly views the woman as Mary as well as the Church. He wants to claim that the mariological interpretation was the earliest in the East. But his reading of Hippolytus is not

compelling; moreover, the influential Greek commentary, that of Andreas of Caesarea (6th–7th century), categorically rejects the identification of the woman with Mary.

5. Cf. Gal. 4:19, a verse used by a number of later interpreters to illuminate Rev. 12.

6. 'No, critical one, you cannot prove that Christ Himself is meant by the child. For, long before the Apocalypse [was written] the Incarnation of the Word took place; but these verses of John concern the present and the future. Moreover, as Christ was born of his mother, he was not suddenly and immediately carried off to the throne of God, out of fear of being attacked by the serpent (Methodius, *Symposium* 8.7; translation from Le Frois, p. 18).

7. Quoted by Le Frois, p. 45.

8. On apocalyptic literature as primarily 'revelatory' rather than 'eschatological', see Christopher Rowland, *The Open Heaven* (London: SPCK, 1982).

9. On this see Leonard L. Thompson, *The Book of Revelation: Apocalypse and Empire* (Oxford: OUP, 1990).

10. For New Testament interpretation of Christ's death and resurrection as a 'birth', see Acts 13:33, quoting Ps.2 (also cited at Rev. 12:5).

11. The interesting parallels between the Woman clothed with the Sun of Rev. 12 and the Woman at the foot of the cross of Jn. 19 are also worthy of note, whether or not one places the Apocalypse firmly within the Johannine stream.

12. Quoted in Ivone Gebara and Maria Clara Bingemer, *Mary; Mother of God, Mother of the Poor* (*Liberation and Theology* 7; Maryknoll, NY: Orbis, 1989), p. 147. These authors provide a distinctively liberationist perspective on the devotion to Our Lady of Guadalupe.

The Built Heritage of the English Church

Timothy Jones

Sir Roy Strong, in his introduction to the book *Change and Decay: The Future of Our Churches*, published to accompany the 1977 Victoria and Albert Museum exhibition, wrote:

> The future of our churches and chapels lies in the coming together to mutual purpose of very different viewpoints. Worshipper, visitor, archaeologist, antiquarian, art historian, architect, restorer, priest, social worker, performer – all these find their focus in the church building and its environs. The concern of such disparate facets of our society is however an inherent force for their preservation

The future of our historic sacred sites, perhaps increasingly, depends upon the coming together of a wide body of interested parties prepared to work in partnership. This partnership may produce an impetus for preservation, restoration or conservation, but it also, most importantly, produces a climate of care for the traditions of our sacred places, recognizing the irreplaceable contributions they have made and must continue to make to our environment. If the built manifestations of our sacred heritage are to grace the future, it is essential to understand the meaning of the historic fabric of the past.

As we await the millennium it is worth remembering that some of the bells which ring it in will ring from a site which was used as a place of worship during the last millennium. An understanding of contemporary society depends to a very considerable degree upon knowledge of and respect for the past, and such knowledge is dependent upon an abundance of primary sources. One of the most important of these sources is often that which is taken for granted – buildings – and one of the most significant building types is the church (or place of worship). The churches, which are a cherished feature of the English landscape, are the earliest above-ground buildings to survive as a group. Sometimes of pre-Norman foundation, they can predate the fortified castles introduced by the Normans and, most significantly, have remained in continuous use, for despite its eye-catching presence, the useful life of a castle for its original purpose was a short one. A church is usually the most striking as well as the most valuable feature of an historic landscape, urban or rural. It has generally survived as for centuries it has been a source of, and focus for, local pride as well as local devotions.

Collectively the parish churches of England are the epitome of, and our most characteristic contribution to Gothic art, and they are centres of art which remain centres of life, whereas the earliest secular buildings now have the status of public monuments; they survive but they lack life. As studies of patronage, churches have from the earliest times been valuable barometers of the distribution of power. Many owe their origins to serving the wider households of Saxon thegns or Norman earls. During the later middle ages, as town life assumed a greater importance, we begin to see the development of parishioners as a body, and initiation of works to a church under the umbrella of guilds. Very often the result was representative of the finest skills, craftsmanship and materials available, and few pre-Renaissance secular buildings match the results. A parish church is one of the best testimonies to the historic prosperity of a town or county, and even when that prosperity has passed away the churches endure as monuments of faith and ambition.

The Henrician and Edwardian Reformations, followed a hundred years later by the iconoclasm of the Puritans, have left a gap in our national artistic heritage as a result of the destruction inflicted upon our places of worship. The late 17th and 18th centuries, with a few exceptional bursts of activity under Charles II and Queen Anne, were largely a period of taking stock, but have bequeathed us a legacy of sacred art by men working in styles as diverse as Hawksmoor at the beginning of the century, to Nash at the end; buildings of European significance. The 18th century receives poor press as an age of faith, yet there runs through this great age of aristocratic self-confidence and emerging mercantile power and prosperity a thread of church building, repairing and adorning. As towns became the resort of polite society the new residential quarters required a fashionable new church, which was often the architectural set piece of any new development. The 19th century, beginning with the establishment of the so-called 'Waterloo churches', was an era of Anglican revival, Catholic and Evangelical, and was the last period of self-confident expansion, aided by the seemingly endless resources of the Industrial Revolution.

But centres of industrial prosperity were often centres of religious dissent, and for the first time the non-conformists began to express their faith architecturally. The presence of so many places of worship (ranging from the chapels of Welsh Methodism to the great monuments of the Roman Catholic revival), are testimonies to the religious and social tolerance which came early to England. Church buildings are therefore a mirror of society; a society which, in the past, valued them as sacred places, and now of a society which although secular, values its past. By striving, for whatever reason, to care for them, we are ensuring that our understanding of previous societies, whose less tangible legacies appear to be withering fast, can continue to develop. A foreign visitor to an English county would, without the help of a guidebook be able to trace the social and economic history of that county by examining its ecclesiastical heritage. They could work out the good times and the bad times from the type and scale of additions (or reductions) and the number and quality of monuments on a church, and changing rituals from the type and quality of its fixtures and fittings. Although the full tide of faith has receded we are still fortunate beyond measure that it has left so rich an inheritance, and that such a high percentage still remains in the use for which it was intended.

Moreover this heritage continues to grow with an understanding and appreciation of the architecture of the post-war years. Insurance money from churches bombed during the last war, for example, was used to construct churches in the new towns and suburbs. Skilled specialist architects like Stephen Dykes Bower and H. S. Goodhart-Rendel, refined the Gothic style, and it was with the building of St Paul's, Bow Common in 1958–60 to the design of Maguire and Murray that the Liturgical Movement, which favoured a central altar, found built expression in England. These new candidates for our sacred places are often found in unexpected places.

It is necessary to stress the value of an item to appreciate the efforts made to ensure its value does not diminish. What then can be done to ensure our sacred places not only survive, but also prosper into and through their second millennium? Practically, with respect to the buildings much has been done and will be done, some of it under the aegis of, and with the support of, secular agents supplementing the unending labours of those who regularly use the buildings. Until comparatively recently, the history of the Church of England is a story of individuals and groups who worshipped in a particular place and were responsible for it. But the wider importance of a church has long been recognized. An antiquarianism which began with Leland was fostered by subsequent scholars and travellers from Defoe to Walpole and Morris, and formulated by societies like the Camden Society, and is as English as Anglicanism itself.

However the idea that a church should enjoy some degree of protection from undesirable change (and decay) is, like all planning issues, a relatively modern one, and the idea that public money should be allocated to this protection is a very modern concept. It might be useful to remind ourselves how the events of the past hundred years have informed the way in which our historic churches are regarded – what indeed constitutes an historic church – and how the experience gained has not only enhanced our appreciation of the past, but in practical terms provided a bedrock to ensure that these places are given an opportunity to survive in a rapidly changing cultural environment.

There is a very beautiful secular place not far from Lincoln College, Oxford, along the Thames at Kelmscott. It is most fitting that this was the residence of William Morris, who, in 1877, aghast at what he considered to be the ruthless works of 'restoration' taking place at Tewkesbury Abbey, founded what was to become the Society for the Protection of Ancient Buildings. In his lifetime, and by the philosophy of his successors, it did much to ensure that when our historic churches are in need of works beyond basic repair and maintenance, that work becomes an intervention stopping short of the radical surgery of 'improvements', which by scrubbing away the patina and accretions of ages can irretrievably erode the special interest of a building. The term 'restoration' when applied to an historic building can be problematical. The term must mean a restoration to the *status quo ante* – but that status may conflict with a philosophy of preservation, to retain the integrity of the structure. It can be argued that working with the existing repairing, replacing and removing only patently unsuitable accretions, best serves the interests of all our historic buildings.

Emerging legislation to protect the historic built environment gained momentum when, in 1912–13, a select committee of Parliament, considering the likely scope of a Bill to safeguard ancient monuments, suggested that churches and cathedrals be included within its remit. However, the Bill as finally passed excluded 'ecclesiastical buildings in ecclesiastical use' (the term still applies). The then Archbishop of Canterbury, Randall Davidson, was prompted to look closely at the means by which the Church could best fulfil its responsibility to its inheritance in an age becoming ever more aware of its less immediate past. (Thomas Cook, as well as guiding tours around our great secular monuments, had early on included churches on his travel itinerary.) By 1938 what is now known as the Diocesan Advisory Committee had been fully established and supported by the Council for the Care of Churches to ensure that stewardship of historic buildings was of an appropriate type. This mechanism was to contrast admirably with the rages of destruction which, even before the last war, were threatening so many historic landmarks.

Until the introduction of the Town and Country Planning Acts of 1944 and 1947, one of the consequences of which was to identify and protect historic buildings, such buildings were scheduled. Now they are 'listed' and the term has become synonymous with historic buildings, although a number of additions to this list are of very recent vintage. The precise implications of what it means for a building to be listed, and why it may be so designated, are set out in an indispensable document issued by the (then) Department of National Heritage and the

Department of Environment (Planning Policy Guidance (PPG) 15). This document provides a full statement of government policies for the identification and protection of the historic environment. The first paragraph of the document is quite unequivocal and particularly relevant to our sacred places. It is worth quoting in full:

> It is fundamental to the Government's policies for environmental stewardship that there should be effective protection for all aspects of the historic environment. The physical survivals of our past are to be valued and protected for their own sake as a central part of our cultural heritage. They are an irreplaceable record which contributes, through formal education and in many other ways, to our understanding of both the present and the past. Their presence adds to the quality of our lives by enhancing the familiar and cherished local scene and sustaining the sense of local distinctiveness which is so important an aspect of our towns, villages and countryside.

Such high and valuable sentiments are given teeth by including buildings which fall into this category on the 'list of buildings of special architectural or historic interest', and it is the duty of the relevant Secretary of State to compile such a list, formally advised by English Heritage. There are three categories within this list: Grades I and II* identify the outstanding architectural or historic interest of perhaps 6 per cent of all listed buildings. The rest, at Grade II, represent a major element in the historic qualities of our cities, towns, villages and countryside. PPG15 continues:

> Once lost, listed buildings cannot be replaced and they can be robbed of their special interest as surely by unsuitable alteration as by outright demolition. The represent a finite resource and an irreplaceable asset.

These are amongst the criteria that any material alteration to a church is likely to be judged.

It is fitting (if not surprising) that so many churches are listed, but whilst a church may be listed it remains exempt from the legal requirement to seek listed building consent for material works. This continuing exemption is dependent, however, upon the operation of an agreed internal system of control, 'The Ecclesiastical Exemption (Listed Buildings and Conservation Areas) Order 1994'. The Church of England shares this privilege (currently under review) with the Church in Wales, the Roman Catholic Church, the Baptist Union, the Methodist Church and the United Reformed Church.

It is important to be aware of the framework by which both sacred and secular bodies become involved in the welfare of our sacred places, and which allows English Heritage as the Government's advisers and agents on the historic built environment to become involved with – some might say trespass into – that significant proportion of the historic built environment which is made up by our churches.

Although the percentage of historic buildings listed at Grades I and II* is very small, in 1993 there were 12,970 listed Anglican churches and perhaps 2,000 listed buildings belonging to other denominations. About 3,000 of the Anglican churches are listed Grade I: 30 per cent of the total of all Grade I listed buildings. Looking at the 65 applications for grant aid received by English Heritage in January 1998, 24 were for churches listed II*, and 20 for churches listed Grade I. Such figures are eloquent witness to the exceptional value of the estate of sacred places and their formal recognition by the state. The Oxford diocese has some 200 Grade I churches and it is rare in any diocese for less than half the places of worship to be listed. In some, Bath and Wells, Lincoln, Norwich, St Edmundsbury and Ipswich for example, up to 90 per cent may be listed, the majority with high grades. Walsingham lies in a region positively cluttered with historic churches – turning one's back on one tower one is frequently confronted with another on the horizon.

These buildings are greedy of maintenance and money and necessary works to the fabric need to be implemented to a particular standard. Until the recent past a church could be largely self-supporting financially, but to care for an historic building without at least occasional outside assistance is beyond the means of many churches. Society values the several roles

played by these buildings to the extent that since the mid 1970s
state aid has been available to the sacred places; a most significant,
encouraging development in the face of an increasingly secular
atmosphere. In 1997 English Heritage celebrated 'England's
Christian Heritage' and for the first time endeavoured to put our
historic churches, chapels, abbeys and cathedrals centre stage.
This was heralded by the building of a new museum on the site
of St Augustine's Abbey, Canterbury (at a cost of £1 million), the
first such project to be undertaken by them. In the course of the
'Christian Heritage Year' grants to cathedrals and churches rose
by £1.8 million to £14.3 million out of a total sum of £41 million
spent on grant aid to all other aspects of the historic environment. Perhaps the most important financial contribution to be
made to places of worship, allowing the millennium to be faced
with greater confidence in the likelihood of projects affecting the
fabric of a church, great and small, coming to fruition, is the
introduction of the heritage Lottery Fund and English Heritage's
'Joint Scheme for Churches and Other Places of Worship'. This
new co-operative approach is designed to ensure that funding
bodies apply their resources in a complementary way, making full
use of the skills and working relationships English Heritage (and
its predecessors) has developed. This funding is currently set at
£20, per annum, to be divided amongst all places of worship of
heritage.

'Significant heritage interest' is the criterion against which
applications for a share of the above funding will be judged. More
practically, this is so if the proposed works are to benefit a
particular historic feature within a churchyard, or if the church
forms the core of a conservation area or settlement, or is a striking
landscape feature, or has special archaeological or antiquarian
interest. The project should also demonstrate a strong
community as well as heritage benefit. This last point raises the
interesting matter of a distinction between funding the fabric of
an historic building or effectively funding those who use such a
building by contributing towards, say, catering facilities, if it can
be demonstrated that the works are essential to the continued use
of the place of worship by extending its use to a wider
community.

The setting of a church, its graveyard and the monuments it contains, its walls and railings are an integral part of a church, and such items can be as significantly graded as the principal listed building.

As important for the well being of the sacred places is the continuing flowering of excellence in craftsmanship, which programmes of repair and restoration encourage. However, a more sensitive issue is a refinement of straightforward allocations of funds in what English Heritage hopes will increasingly be a working partnership between the agents for grant aid and its recipient. The fabric of an historic church may be sound and enhanced as a result of works supported by fundraising and grant aid, but such works should be carried out to a building in a manner which is viable and sustainable. Few of our historic churches will have reached the millennium unchanged since their consecration and this process of evolution, particularly with reference to their interiors, continues. It is perhaps shortsighted to provide funds for a major 'heritage' project if the congregation of a church is unhappy with what they might see as constraints imposed by aspects of the historic fabric they have inherited. As with all listed buildings, it is of paramount importance to keep them in the use for which they were intended.

Churches, like other distinct groups of historic buildings (for example, agricultural buildings) can lose much of their special interest architecturally and atmospherically, when converted to other uses. Rather than allow a congregation to abandon a church, an intelligent and imaginative approach needs to be adopted towards any emerging proposals for change, which most commonly can range from the removal of fixtures and fittings which dictate a particular form of worship, to the introduction of buildings within buildings to provide new services. Faced with such proposals it is vital that all interested parties identify what constitutes the special interest of a listed building, and what degree of change can be effected without eroding that special interest. There will always be some sacred places whose architectural value is so great that little, if any change can be contemplated, but more often degrees of change can be considered.

English Heritage has published *New Work in Historic Churches* and the gist of the advice it contains is to suggest that, when change takes place, nothing of value is lost irretrievably. Whilst re-ordering is the most headline grabbing aspect of works to a church (and is usually assumed to be the main reason for internal changes in churches), in practice it usually forms part of a wider programme of work to which the same considerations apply; ultimate reversibility. Certainly within the diocese of London, where a named English Heritage representative regularly attends meetings of the Diocesan Advisory Committee, there is the opportunity to comment from an historic buildings perspective at an early stage of the development of proposals. This may or may not generate an application for funding and provides such information as may be necessary for a fully informed discussion on the particular aspects of an historic building.

In inner cities the problems facing churches can be acute. The social issues of a dwindling urban population, a rapid turnover of residents with little sense of focus or loyalty, and those who leave the city for a country retreat each weekend, or the architectural legacy of too many churches, indicate that current patterns of settlement can be very different from those of a hundred years ago.

The north western parts of Westminster in London, for example, appear to experience many of these urban trends where there is a core of regular worshippers resident near to their place of worship, who find that the scale of such places no longer reflects the scale of the congregation. These early suburbs boasted fine churches, built to attract new residents to a speculative development and were frequently the first and finest building, acting as a social and architectural focus. The fashionable life of these early suburbs (which we would now regard as being inner city) was often short, as improved communications allowed their residents to move further and further from the centre, leaving the church stranded in the midst of a very different population than that it was designed to serve. These buildings may have enjoyed only several decades of prosperity before the long slow decline began, with fatal consequences for the fabric.

A church, which was erected in the 1850s as a picturesque

adornment to Westbourne Park, Paddington, falls neatly into this category. Listed Grade II, it is a typical Victorian building on an island site. After decades of dwindling congregations the church was finally closed after being declared unsafe. Even the most basic works of repair and maintenance, inside and out, had not been carried out and the appearance was one of desolation and neglect, which increased the longer the church was not in use. English Heritage, working closely with the Diocese of London, was keen to explore along with the interest of local community groups, proposals for an alternative use. Suggestions ranged from office or educational use, to an arts or community centre. The obstacles to such proposals proved insurmountable, largely due to the cost of essential works of repair and maintenance, and the spectre of at least partial demolition loomed. However, a saviour appeared in the form of Holy Trinity, Brompton, who were prepared to restore the church and reopen it for services again. The consequences for the interior of the church were considerable as a result of changed patterns of worship, but the alternative was a stark one. The special architectural interest of this church was concentrated largely in its townscape value and internal spatial qualities. The internal fixtures and fittings could be amended without eroding the special interest and many items salvaged for re-use. The considerable works to the fabric were put in hand with help from one of the first London schemes to take up funding, and the work was monitored by English Heritage. Now a thriving and well-maintained church continues to make a valuable architectural and spiritual contribution to the life of a community, partly due to a flexible partnership between the sacred and secular. It is a tremendously encouraging marker for the millennium.

But what of secular use for sacred places? Given the presumption in favour of the preservation of listed buildings, if continuing ecclesiastical use is not possible, alternative uses must be explored to save the place, if not its purpose. The issue is a sensitive one, but sensitive uses and sensitive interventions can be found, resulting in an historic church saved for our architectural heritage, if not our sacred community.

In 1976 the Church Commissioners had approved the

demolition of one church every nine days – 39 in the course of a year. In its Annual Report for 1975, the Advisory Board of Redundant Churches forecast that by 1986 over 1,000 churches would have been declared redundant, and that thereafter the redundancy rate would be either maintained or increased. Let us hope that this nadir has passed.

There will continue to be casualties; such casualties have characterized worship in England. But let us hope that the awareness of the issues raised in this essay will allow us to enter the millennium still surrounded by evidence of past worship, and to step out of our everyday secular world into a wealth of well-maintained churches. These churches form one of our most precious legacies, which all interested parties will have to continue to cherish. What use we find for the buildings of this inheritance is an open question. Let us hope that they will be handed on in a condition of physical dignity to accord with the sacred ritual for which they were built, but without conferring museum status upon them.

Music and Devotion to Our Lady in the Anglican Tradition

Colin Baldy

Even a fairly cursory glance at the music lists of most of our great cathedrals, greater parish churches and collegiate foundations will, these days, reveal a large amount of music in honour of Our Lady. *Ave Marias* by Bruckner, Cornysh, Rachmaninov, Parsons and many others abound. A whole gamut of Marian texts from the *Salve Regina* to *tota pulchra est* is represented by composers as diverse as Herbert Howells, Duruflé, Tavener, Morales and Stravinsky. Perhaps Deans and Provosts, and their respective Directors of Music, have been converted wholesale to devotion to Mary. Maybe there is now a willingness to accord much more importance to the Marian feasts contained in the Lectionary. Or perhaps it is just that so much beautiful music exists in honour of the Mother of God. Certainly, this situation would have been unthinkable until quite recently. Indeed there have been at least two grave periods in the history of our Church when the use of music in worship at all was called into question.

Before the Reformation, devotion to Mary had assumed a cult status in England. Those who pay honour to Our Lady at Walsingham are well-acquainted with the description of England as Our Lady's dowry. The little office to Our Lady contained within the Book of Hours was one of the most popular private devotions of the time, and it was customary, after the Office of Compline, to process to a statue or altar to Mary to sing one of the Marian anthems. Music for such occasions is contained within the Eton, Caius and Lambeth choir books, and in the Peterhouse part books, themselves copied from those at Magdalen College, Oxford.[1] Indeed, the statutes of Eton College specify that this act of devotion before a shrine to Our Lady shall be carried out daily. It even specifies the music which should be sung.[2]

All this did not change overnight. In the break with Rome,

Henry VIII was more concerned with the position of the secular
authority in relation to the ecclesiastical authority than with the
niceties of liturgy. In this he was no different from Henry II in his
quarrels with Thomas à Becket. Unfortunately, his timing was
not good; those who had been influenced by the teachings of the
Protestant reformers on the continent saw the opportunity to
pursue their aims in an English Church no longer shackled to
Rome. A century of sometimes violent change and compromise
followed. Henry, of course, considered himself a good Catholic.
This was not the case with his son, Edward VI who, having been
instructed by Protestant tutors was then put at the mercy of the
Lord Protectors, Somerset and Northumberland. Under
Somerset's auspices, the 1549 Book of Common Prayer was
issued. Even then, the English Church did not become severely
Protestant along the continental model. Following Henry's break
with Rome, three primers issued in 1534, 1539 and 1545 had all
contained the *Ave Maria*, albeit without its second half ('Holy
Mary, Mother of God') and, as John Milburn states in his paper
'Mary in Tudor Anglican Writings', given to the Pontificia
Academia Mariana Internationalis in 1979[3] there was no denial
of the doctrines of Mary's immaculate nature in the new Prayer
Book or in articles and homilies of the time. The Christmas Day
collect in the 1552 Book of Common Prayer includes the words:

> Almighty God, which has given us thy only-begotten Son to
> take our nature upon Him, and this day to be born of a pure
> virgin . . .

Similar sentiments are contained within the Proper Preface for
the day. The catechism of 1553 states that:

> the seed (as St Paul doth plainly teach) is Jesus Christ, the Son
> of God, very god and very man; conceived of the Holy Ghost;
> engendered of the womb and substance of Mary, the blessed
> pure and undefiled Maid . . .

At the same time, ideas about the proper conduct of the services
contained within the new Prayer Book were being circulated.

John Merbecke published his *The book of Common Praier Noted* in 1550 and, as the imprint makes clear, this was with the full authority of both Cranmer and the Lord Protector, who was by this time, Northumberland. According to the wishes of the Archbishop, Merbecke seems to have followed the premise that 'in mine opinion, the song that shall be made thereunto would not be full of notes, but, as near as may be, for every syllable a note'.[4] In the Communion Service, the Preface is detailed to be sung on a monotone, although there are quite complicated settings for the Offertory and the other parts of the Mass. None of this is, however, as florid as the plainsong which it replaced, with its extended melismas and cadences.

As far as the Offices in Merbecke's book are concerned, the chants for both the canticles and the psalms are very obviously based on those of the Sarum rite. Nearly fifty years later, one of his successors at the Chapel Royal, Thomas Morley did the same in his 1597 book *A Plaine and Easie Introduction to Practicall Musicke*.[5] Morley, however, goes on to add faux-bourdens to the chants, in effect harmonizing them, with the tune in the tenor. Slightly later still, Adrian Batten, who was active in the period before the Civil War (he died in 1637), similarly harmonized chants and was, to all intents and purposes, writing what we now call Anglican chant.

Even had Edward VI lived, it is doubtful that he would have swept away the order which a regulated prayer book lent not only to public acts of worship in his kingdom, but to the very running of the realm. This practical consideration flew in the face of his more radical teachers and advisers who, influenced by the teachings of Zwingli and Calvin, would have preferred a more extempore model. Fortunately, the continued use of a prayer-book enabled composers to carry on writing and developing their musical ideas.

This development of ideas led, over time, to the practice of composing special settings of Preces and Responses and of the Canticles for festal occasions. This was very largely helped by the conduct of services in Elizabeth I's Chapel Royal. Here we need to look, briefly, at what has become known as the 'Elizabethan Settlement'. Although educated by the same Protestant tutors as her brother, Elizabeth certainly did not want to be 'hectored by godly presbyters'[6] along the Scottish model. Nor did she want to give up the headship of the Church and accept the possible loss of the throne, which a continued allegiance to Rome might have led to; in the Pope's eyes, Elizabeth was a bastard. In her *middle way* the queen managed to ensure both the continuance of the choral foundations, and the place of music in the services within her new Prayer Book, issued in 1559; and this contrary to the wishes of those Protestants who hoped to banish music altogether. Peter Le Huray, in his book *Music and the Reformation in England* quotes the 1559 visitation to administer the oath of supremacy as saying:

> ... the Queen's Majesty, neither meaning in any wise the decay of anything that might conveniently tend to the use and continuance of the said science [*i.e. music*], neither to have the same in any way abused in the church, that thereby the common prayer should be the worse understood of the hearers, willeth and commandeth, that first no alteration be made of such assignments of living that heretofore have been appointed to the use of singing or music in the church, but that the same so remain.[7]

Having established the place of music in her Prayer Book, Elizabeth was free to enjoy the same in the company of all manner of pomp and spectacle. Le Huray quotes the secretary to the Duke of Württemberg on a visit to the Chapel Royal at Windsor:

> The music, and especially the organ, was exquisite. At times could be heard cornets, then flutes, then recorders and other instruments. And there was a little boy who sang so sweetly, ornamenting the music in such a way with this little tongue that it was really wonderful to listen to him. Their ceremonies indeed are very similar to those of the papists ...

Although the situation was markedly different elsewhere in the Church, the great flowering of artistic endeavour, both musical and otherwise, which such patronage facilitated, reached its apotheosis in the Caroline Church. By this time the view of the Church of England as an English Catholic Church shorn of the excesses of the continental variety, was well established and vast amounts of music by composers such as Orlando Gibbons, Thomas Tomkins and William Child were written to beautify its services.

Returning to John Milburn, this time in a later paper given in Rome entitled 'Maria restituta'[8] he makes the point that during this period we once more find writings and icons to Our Lady. John Donne, in part five of *The Litanie* writes

> For that fair blessed Mother-Maid,
> Whose flesh redeem'd us . . .
> Our zealous thanks we pour.
> As her deeds were our helps,
> So are her prayers;
> Nor can she sue in vain,
> Who hath such titles unto you

And we should not miss the opportunity of mentioning the famous statue to Our Lady erected, during William Laud's period as Chancellor of Oxford University, above the door to the University Church in 1637; nor of a similar statue of about the same period in the quad of Oriel College.

Later in the same century we find Bishop Kenn (1637–1711) writing on the Immaculate Conception and the Assumption. The lines on the former run,

> The Holy Ghost His temple in her built,
> Cleansed from congenial, kept from mortal guilt;
> And from the moment that her blood was fired
> Into her heart celestial love inspired.

Of course, it wasn't all plain sailing as far as these High Church practices were concerned. The fate of Archbishop Laud is well known, and others, too, had problems. One Peter Smart subjected Dean Cosin at Durham to a lawsuit in the 1620s who, complaining about the conduct of the Eucharist in the cathedral, said:

> ... when men's minds should be occupied about heavenly meditations about Christ's bitter death and passion, of their own sins; of faith and repentance ... at that very season, most unseasonably, their ears are possessed with pleasant tunes, and their eyes fed with pompous spectacles of glittering pictures and histrionical gestures ...[9]

On the whole, however, practices which would have been unthinkable a mere fifty years before were able to flourish. Indeed the queen, Henrietta Maria, was able to attend Catholic Mass publicly in her chapel, having three priests in her service who were able to function quite unhindered.[10] This did not continue, however, because the Civil War came along, and both the king and the archbishop lost their heads. The years that followed were terrible times for both musicians and clerics. C.V. Wedgwood, in her excellent book *The King's War*, details some very harrowing accounts of clergy and their families forced into penury as a result of the visitations instituted by parliament on 'scandalous ministers'.[11]

With the Restoration came an initial resurgence of activity. John Blow and Henry Purcell were, of course, active at this time, but Milburn points out that High Church enthusiasm in the Church of England seems to have gone out of it.[12] The century which followed was the low-water mark of the Church of England, both liturgically and musically, though notable composers like Boyce, Croft and Crotch were exceptions to this.

Apart from settings of the Magnificat, no Marian music had been composed in England probably since William Byrd published his *Gradualia* in 1605 and 1607. However, just when foundlings were being required to repay the charity of their parishes by singing in church, and the parish clerk was required to keep the congregation in time, Samuel Wesley started composing wonderful Latin motets. Despite being the nephew of the founder of Methodism, Wesley converted to Roman Catholicism in 1784, having been, as he put it, 'seduced by their Gregorian

Chants'.[13] He wrote a large number of Marian motets and we can safely include him in our review since, in later life, having also composed much Anglican service music, he denied the conversion ever having taken place. This was probably untrue, but in any case the Church of England is nothing, if not eclectic, and has always been willing to draw on the best of all traditions, certainly in modern times.

Wesley may appear to have been flying in the face of fashion, but a major upheaval was about to bring him almost into the mainstream. The Oxford Movement was of major importance to renewal in the Church of England, and most people are familiar with the aesthetic effects of the movement on its buildings. Think for a moment of all those restored and rebuilt chancels, and of the organs that were installed in them alongside robed choirs. It was not long before even quite modest churches were able to muster choirs to sing the Offices of Mattins and Evensong. On a grander scale, the church of St John the Divine, Kennington had such a large number of singers before the war that it was able to field either a decani or cantoris choir to sing the Office every day of the week. There was, however, no choral foundation as at All Saints, Margaret Street. At St John's, as at other city churches, men and boys would arrive after work to sing to the glory of God within the Anglican prayer book tradition.

What sort of music would they have sung? A certain amount of Tudor and Jacobean music for the Offices of Mattins and Evensong had been kept alive in the cathedrals. We can be fairly sure, however, that performances left a lot to be desired and contemporary settings of an inferior nature were really the norm, although Samuel Wesley's son, Samuel Sebastian, undertook a lot of work to improve the situation. There had been a tendency within some circles to accept anything, so long as it was music. Fortunately, the renaissance in church building corresponded with a renaissance in English church music.

Stanford was one of the foremost composers in this movement. He and many others contributed an enormous amount of high quality music to the repertoire, and now, with the easy accessibility of recorded and broadcast music, there is a much greater use of this resource. It is not unusual to hear choirs around the country attempting music by John Tavener and Benjamin Britten. People like what they hear, and want a chance to sing it for themselves.

Choral music for the Eucharist took longer to make the crossover from cathedrals and Anglo-Catholic parishes to the mainstream Church of England, largely because the Eucharist was not accorded the place in public worship that it now occupies. Much of the eucharistic music which does come to us from the second half of the 19th century is difficult to programme now because, following the Prayer Book practice of the time, it usually contains responses to the commandments rather than a three, six or nine-fold Kyrie, no Agnus Dei, and a very extended Gloria, to be sung at the end. Anglo-Catholics rediscovered Merbecke. It was really the important work of R.R. Terry at Westminster Cathedral earlier in the 20th century which led to a rediscovery of the glories of renaissance music for the Mass. The sort of singing which was now heard at Westminster was totally different from the tradition which English ears has become accustomed to in Anglican cathedrals, and inspired Herbert Howells to compose what was possibly the first Mass setting by an Englishman since William Byrd. In 1923 Terry commissioned Ralph Vaughan Williams to write a Mass for him and his choir. The result was a stunning Mass in G, which combines the form of Tudor choral music with Vaughan Williams' own modal style.

At the time of composition, Vaughan Williams never expected it to be heard in the Church of England, certainly not in Latin at any rate. It is really the Parish Mass movement and the corresponding liturgical changes that have allowed such music, along with 16th-century settings, once more to be sung in the Anglican Church.

As far as music to Our Lady is concerned, a number of Anglican religious orders re-instituted the practice of singing the Marian anthems after compline. In one instance, the Community of St Mary the Virgin at Wantage has played a very important part in the rediscovery of plainsong within the Anglican Church. Apart from the motets of Wesley, and those of Sir Edward Elgar, there has been little choral music of a specifically Marian nature composed until relatively recently. It is fortunate that contemporary composers are no longer frightened to set Marian texts. Benjamin Britten wrote his *A Hymn to the Virgin* whilst he was still at school, and only 17 years old. He had found the anonymous 14th-century poem at the beginning of his copy of the Oxford Book of Verse, which he had just won as a school prize. John Tavener is a convert to the Russian Orthodox Church in which devotion to Mary has an important place. He has accepted commissions for several items of Anglican music, and his *Hymn to the Mother of God*, whilst strictly Orthodox, fits well into Anglican worship, and looking further back, once again R.R. Terry brought the enormous wealth of music from earlier centuries to our notice.

In the area of hymnody things have been somewhat different. A large number of Marian hymns have, of course, been employed in Anglo-Catholic parishes since the early days. Some of them were ancient, and were eventually put into print by the English Hymnal in 1916.[14] Others were rather sentimental, borrowed from the hymns and poems from the very earliest days. There is a splendid processional using the Lourdes melody, which appears in *The Visitation* 1929 edition. In the Autumn 1968 edition Father Turner Cole contributed an interesting article on Marian Hymns, entitled 'Explaining Our Lady'.

The movement of the Church of England towards liturgical models common within the rest of the Catholic Church has enabled an eclecticism to be applied liberally where music for the Eucharist is concerned. This has also had an effect on music for the Offices.

It has been a long and often painful journey to the present position. Cranmer can little have thought that his conflation of Vespers and Compline, the Evensong, would inspire so much beauty, and we should rejoice in it. But we should also rejoice that the very nature of the Church of England enables us to use so much of what is good from other traditions. Let us raise a glass, then, to more *Ave Marias* and *Regina Coelis* on cathedral music lists.

Notes

1. J. Wainwright, *Composers, Church and State in Sixteenth Century England*. The Open University. Course AA302 *From composers to performers*, 1998.
2. J. Milsom, *The flower of all virginity*. Music from the Eton Choir Book, Volume 4. The Sixteen Under Harry Christophers. Collins Classics, 1952.
3. J. Milburn, *Mary in Tudor Anglican Writings*. Pontifica Academia Mariana Internationalis, 1979.
4. J. Stevens, Preface to the 1979 facsimile edition of Merbecke's *The booke of Common Praier noted*. Nottingham Court Press and Magdalen College, Cambridge, 1979.
5. T. Morley, *A Plaine and Easie Introduction to Practicall Musicke* (1597), ed. R. A. Harman, 1952.
6. J. A. Cannon, *Elizabeth I*, The Oxford Companion to British History, 1997.
7. P. Le Huray, *Music and the Reformation in England, 1549–1660*, Cambridge University Press, 1978.
8. J. Milburn, *Maria restituta: an episode of Seventeenth Century Anglicanism*, Pontifica Academia Mariana Internationalis, 1983.
9. As note 7.
10. J. P. Kenyon, *The Stuarts*, Fontana/Collins, 1966.
11. C. V. Wedgwood, *The King's War*, William Collins & Sons, 1958.
12. As note 8.
13. Article on Samuel Wesley in *Grove's Dictionary of Music and Musicians*, 1929.
14. *The English Hymnal*, Oxford University Press 1916. Revised 1933.

Cathedrals: Sacred Spaces and Common Ground

Stephen Platten

At the heart of the Gospel is the life, teaching, passion, death and resurrection of Jesus. For it was Jesus' teaching, and the life He lived, that convicted people of the truth that in Him God had spoken and, indeed, had walked this earth. Some years ago one theologian expressed the essence of this Gospel thus:

> That life is grace to us, our own lives and the lives of all those we encounter, that all things great and small are gift, the treasure we can at any moment discover, the banquet to which all are equally invited. No delay must mar this discovery nor decline the invitation, for such ingratitude instantly ungraces us; it is that life is more than bread, more than accumulated possessions; it is also to realise that the true value of someone or something and to discover treasure, are one and the same imperative act. Finally, that the true value of all that exists is discovered in the unique way in which one values a gift; that we should therefore not crush by grasping, or tear by trying to pull away.[1]

Central to the Gospel, then, is the word 'grace'. It refers to that which is freely given. The most scandalous part of Jesus' teaching and his life was its unconditional nature. Perhaps nowhere else now are there *buildings* which quite so powerfully express that unconditional nature of the Gospel than our cathedrals.

> Sir Gilbert [Lewis] . . . said mad people are apt to come to Cathedrals. There was a mad woman who came to Worcester Cathedral and gave him a great deal of trouble by screeching out. There was a Mr Quarrell who used to make antics at the time of the Communion. At a certain point in the service this man would bow down till he got his head on the pavement and his movements were so extraordinary that all they could

do was to look at him and watch him. The authorities did not
know what to do with him. They could not say, 'You shall not
be a Communicant', but they let him know indirectly that
they thought his proceedings very ridiculous. 'Ah,' said Sir
Gilbert, 'you don't know all the little games that go on in
Cathedrals.'[2]

Despite all this he was not thrown out of the building. There are
contemporary parallels. Margaret remains a frequent visitor to
one of our cathedrals. She brings her dog in with her and
encourages him to sing; she has had her previous four dogs
stuffed and keeps them at home on her houseboat. Fred divides
his day between the waiting room at the main railway station and
the cathedral. Frequently he will have conversations in the
cathedral with the diocesan bishop; on one occasion, since the
bishop made no attempt to reply, Fred threw his breakfast at
him. The diocesan bishop died in 1837; Fred was talking to a
monument!

These unusual people come regularly to our cathedrals simply
because they are places of shelter, refuge or sanctuary. But there
is, of course, much more to it than that. There is about most
cathedrals a very clear sense of *place*. At the most trivial level this
may simply relate to their being the local landmark. The tower,
the spire or the lantern dominates the city. But there is more to it
still. A cathedral is also seen as a place endowed with a particular
aura of holiness; it is 'sacred space'.

The classical point of departure in marking off the particu-
larity of a cathedral as a sacred *place*, is the association of the
bishop with the building. Cathedrals are not simply large
churches. A cathedral would not be a cathedral were it not for the
presence in the building of the bishop's *cathedra* or chair. From
the patristic period onward the cathedral was built with this in
mind. The pattern out of which this grew was basilican. The *Aula
Palatina* in Trier, a secular building, is a good example. Built by
Constantine the Great, it was used by the local Roman prefect
and consists of a rectangular building with an apsidal end. At the
centre of the apse would have sat the prefect, surrounded by his
college of advisers. This pattern was adopted by the Christian

Church. Some cathedrals have preserved this pattern. The Romanesque building in Norwich still contains the bishop's *cathedra* in its ancient position, high up in the eastern apse.

The position of the eastern *cathedra* in Norwich, elevated at the top of a flight of steps, focuses a further point about the essential nature of a cathedral. It is the *place* within which the teaching role of the bishop is focused. This tradition has been rediscovered and re-vitalized in recent years by Carlo-Maria Martini, the Cardinal Archbishop of Milan; a formidable series of teaching seminars, lectures and courses has restored the great cathedral in Milan to its former role, a role which, in that place, reaches back to the time of St Ambrose in the late 4th century. It is a tradition that cathedrals and bishops can and ought to rediscover.

But the influence of the bishop in his cathedral extends beyond teaching alone in at least two other directions. First, bishops built cathedrals to *focus the presence of the divine*. From earliest times this was inextricably bound into an understanding of a cathedral as a shrine. Where an episcopal basilica was established over the grave of a noted saint, the connection is obvious. The classical example is St Peter's, Rome; the excavation of the site of the tomb of St Peter has helped recapture a tradition that is now less immediate for many Christians. But this association with the saints was very powerful indeed during the period of the early church. Peter Brown summarizes this well. Reflecting on Hegel's discussion of piety and the holy in the medieval period, he writes:

> in the cult of the relics also, late-antique and early mediaeval piety lived down with gusto to his [Hegel's] strictures. This cult gloried in particularity. *Hic locus est*: 'Here is the place', or simply *hic*, is a refrain that runs through the inscriptions on the early martyrs' shrines of North Africa. The holy was available in one *place* [my italics], and in each such place it was accessible to one group in a manner in which it could not be accessible to anyone situated elsewhere.[3]

It was a matter, then, of focusing the presence of God in a particular place. The significance of such a localized focus grew and became the centre of medieval pilgrimages: St James at

Compostela, St Boniface at Fulda and St Cuthbert at Durham are three classical examples. In later medieval times this developed still further, and the shrine of Thomas à Becket in Canterbury is perhaps the most celebrated case in England. Essential to the early development of this tradition, then, was the role of the bishop. Indeed the prestige and power of the bishop might well be enhanced by such a development.

> Furthermore, building and ceremonial at such shrines would sum up more appositely than anywhere else the paradox of episcopal wealth ... such wealth and ceremonial would be deployed in the invisible presence of a figure who had taken on all the features of a later Roman *patronus*. The saint was the good *patronus*; he was the *patronus* whose intercessions were successful, whose wealth was at the disposal of all, whose *potentia* was exercised without violence and to whom loyalty could be shown without constraint. The bishop could stand for him.[4]

The setting of the saint's shrine within the bishop's church brought together different focuses of the holy. Even where there is no shrine, relics could impart a sacred presence. In Norwich, beneath the ancient eastern bishop's throne is a reliquary niche. It reaches back to the beginnings of the cathedral and has always been a place of great holiness. From the ceiling of the niche emerges a 'flue' which makes its way up to the floor beneath the bishop's feet. From the relic, God's spirit is made present to each succeeding bishop in his ministry.

The second direction of episcopal influence in cathedrals is effectively *ecclesiological*. The cathedral is an ecclesiological focus, because the bishop himself is the focus of unity for the Church in that county or region. While the Church of God remains divided the truth of this phrase 'focus of unity' is obviously compromised. Nevertheless it is upon this notion of episcopacy that most theological dialogue aimed at visible unity has been based. It is on the office of bishop that unity should centre; the bishop's ministry is one of those aspects of the life of the Church that holds Christians together in communion with each other in one

place. Hence the presence of two bishops in one locality empha-
sizes the damaging disunity which still persists.

In being the focus of unity for a particular locality, however, it
is the bishop who also makes possible the links of the local church
with the universal. As the Church developed the need arose for
oversight. The episcopate came to fulfil this function, with priests
acting as focuses within smaller eucharistic communities; the
eucharist within which they presided was still the bishop's
eucharist, that is, it still associated itself with the universal
Church through the wider focal ministry of the bishop. The
bishop was also part of a wider college of episcopal oversight. It
was this college that would assume the role of handing on the
teaching of the 'Catholic Church'.

This pattern of collegiality and universality means that
cathedrals themselves become signs of the wider Church. They are
there to remind all who come of the wider community of
Christians throughout the world. In the work of the Anglican–
Roman Catholic International Commission, and through the
visits of successive Archbishops of Canterbury to Rome, a still
wider collegiality has been identified. Archbishop Runcie, in his
visit to Pope John Paul II in 1989, said: 'could not all Christians
come to reconsider the kind of Primacy the bishop of Rome
exercised within the early Church, a "presiding in love" for the
sake of the unity of the Churches in the diversity of their mission?'[5]

None of this can have any reality without the symbolic
presence of bishops in each locality. That presence is made visible
through the existence of cathedrals. The presence and role of
bishops, then, is essential in any theological understanding of
cathedrals. This is the more obvious when we view a cathedral in
its sacramental role. On Maundy Thursday, the diocesan bishop
gathers together his clergy for the Blessing of the Oils. Often this
is accompanied by the clergy re-affirming their episcopal, priestly
and diaconal vows. At Easter, the ancient custom of the bishop
baptising and confirming in his cathedral at the time of the
paschal celebrations is beginning to be recovered. The bishop also
frequently celebrates the eucharist in his cathedral at the great
feasts of Easter, Christmas and Pentecost. This celebration of the
great sacraments of salvation means that cathedrals proclaim the

Christian message of redemption, and so have a prophetic role within contemporary society; indeed this same proclamation of the sacraments of salvation happens continuously through the daily and weekly ministry of the cathedral. Cathedrals remain then the sacred *places par excellence* of the Christian sacraments.

Alongside this sacramental focus there has also been an ancient tradition of daily prayer and the saying of the Office from earliest times. A cathedral is also a *place* that honours the rhythm of each day in a sustained pattern of prayer. One of the main roots of the daily Office stems from the so-called 'cathedral office'. It was described as the cathedral office to mark it off from the daily hours of prayer honoured in the monasteries. The key factor about the cathedral office was its public nature. Instead of resonating with the monastic patterns of seven hours of prayer, cathedrals resonated with the natural rhythms of daybreak and dusk. From the beginning, the public Office in cathedrals took advantage of the fact that they were large city churches. They offered music, drama and the participation of the people. One of the key factors was that in the early tradition of the cathedral office there were no books; instead the people were encouraged to participate with the use of repeated antiphons, responses and refrains. It was the cathedrals that preserved this practice for the longest period of time. George Guiver notes: 'At Lincoln in the fifteenth century no-one was allowed in choir with a book, save for the dean, precentor, chancellor and treasurer. In France, the council of Narbonne in 1551 forbade the canons to have any book in choir with them, even a personal breviary.'[6] Prayer was thus rooted in the sacred space of the cathedral rather than in the proliferation of books which so easily diverted the impulse into the private spiritual lives of each individual. In the eastern church, something of this same pattern is still traceable in the corporate singing of countless litanies in Orthodox Vespers.

Interestingly enough it was effectively the cathedral model that Cranmer revived in his transformation of the Office into the twice daily pattern of Morning and Evening Prayer. The pattern which issued from Cranmer's revision was exactly that of honouring the opening and the closing of the day with a daily rhythm of prayer. The collects of Matins and Evensong set the scene precisely: 'O Lord our heavenly father, almighty and ever-living God, which has safely brought us to the beginning of this day', and 'Lighten our darkness, we beseech thee, O Lord, and by thy great mercy defend us from all perils and dangers of this night'. Although, admittedly, it had been from the monastic hours that Cranmer had culled the material for his new Offices, it was the cathedral pattern that was to emerge. Furthermore, Cranmer's aim had been precisely to restore the public recitation of the Office and to encourage the laity to join the minister in this pattern of daily prayer. In the event, through a process of historical development, it has been the cathedrals that have come closest to Cranmer's ideal. This has been due both to the expectations placed upon cathedrals and the resources available to them. In every English cathedral, the evening Office will be *sung* at least once (in almost every case more than once) per week. Both Morning and Evening Prayer will be said daily and publicly. Often a sprinkling of devout lay people and occasional visitors will join the clergy.

From early times, then, the theological rationale which has underpinned cathedrals has brought together a mixture of the incarnational and redemptive aspects of the Christian Gospel. In their regular performance of the great sacraments they have proclaimed to the world the saving grace of the one who, in giving himself, offered resurrection and new life to all humanity. At the same time, the universality of God's grace through Christ's incarnation has been proclaimed by the presence of the bishop's chair at the heart of a cathedral, and by the public recitation of the divine Office. Each of these is offered to a wider world so that a cathedral may become a focus which draws 'all sorts and conditions of people'.

If cathedrals were originally built as the great churches to enshrine the bishop's throne, in contemporary times they have become so much more than this. Now so many come: pilgrims come seeking out a shrine – the martyrdom of Becket at Canterbury, the shrine of Cuthbert in Durham or of Hugh at Lincoln are places hallowed by prayer – under the shrine at Lincoln the pavement is hollowed out by the countless knees that have bowed in prayer to the memory of the holy man over the centuries. Then there are seekers who know that they are on a journey towards some greater reality but are not yet quite sure how to express that truth; some of these will leave in inchoate sentences their prayers on the cards by the votive candles; some will engage a priest in conversation or coyly avoid him as they make their way quietly through the cathedral. Thirdly, there are those of no faith but who still realize that they can step unhindered into such a building; they are drawn by the power of its vision. Then there are the weary and the sad who come to the Cathedral as did the travellers of old.

Let me end by giving some substance to each of these visions. I shall leave the pilgrims, having focused on them earlier.

First there are the seekers. These are clearly captured in Philip Toynbee's poignant autobiography *Part of a Journey*. Toynbee came to Christianity very late in life, having been fairly militantly anti-Christian. It is his description of dropping into Peterborough Cathedral at the time of Evensong, and before his religious conversion, that expresses the heart of the seeker so clearly:

There is something in every cathedral to take the breath away, and at Peterborough this comes as soon as you set your eyes on the amazing west front with its three huge and equal portals. A notice on the porch door told us that Evensong had already begun and would we please sit down until it was over. If we wished to join the service we could take our seats in the choir . . . we compromised by sitting down on the foremost nave pew but one. Choir, congregation and priests seemed to be islanded there . . . and although we were familiar with Anglican liturgies it was impossible to feel that we were fully part of those proceedings in the unknown cathedral. The service came to an end . . . and we got up from our places to make our circumambulation of the cathedral, guide book in hand. By now this episode has compelled my imagination many ways and driven my mind in several different directions. But the dominant impression which remains is of a gracious, holy but esoteric ceremony being performed in the choir at Peterborough, massively isolated from the modern city outside . . . And yet we had not been only spectators of that deft performance; so far as each of us had found it possible we had also been participants. And if we had arrived five minutes earlier we would have certainly accepted the invitation to take two of those vacant places in the choir stalls. For certainly we both belonged – wholly in spirit and largely in faith – with what was being celebrated in Peterborough Cathedral on that Saturday afternoon at the tail end of the football season.[7]

Then there are the non-believers. They are classically captured in Philip Larkin's well-known poem *Church-Going*. In that poem Larkin is not referring to cathedrals particularly, but more likely the parish churches throughout our land. Nevertheless the attitudes which he conjures up and which are part of his own life would equally apply to the non-believers and indeed to some of the tourists who have not yet thought about belief as they enter a cathedral. He was not sure whether to stop and step in:

> Yet stop I did: in fact I often do,
> And always end much at a loss like this,
> Wondering what to look for; wondering, too,
> When churches fall completely out of use
> What we shall turn them into, if we shall keep
> A few cathedrals chronically on show,
> Their parchment, plate and pyx in locked cases,
> And let the rest rent-free to rain and sheep,
> Shall we avoid them as unlucky places?

Later he reflects that:

> A serious house on serious earth it is,
> In whose blent air all our compulsions meet,
> Are recognised, and robed as destinies.
> And that much never can be obsolete,
> Since someone will for ever be surprising
> A hunger in himself to be more serious,
> And gravitating with it to this ground,
> Which, he once heard, was proper to grow wise in,
> If only that so many dead lie round[8]

Finally there are the weary, the sad and those who come for
sustenance. This returns us to the Gospel of grace where I began.
Here I leave you with a reflection by one who later indeed
became the Dean of Canterbury. It is Dick Sheppard's vision of
St Martins-in-the-Fields. Returning broken after characteristi-
cally wearing himself out tending the sick and dying in the First
World War, he describes those people who had fallen within his
care as they look into the church:

> I stood on the west steps, and saw what this church would be
> to the life of the people. There passed me, into its warm inside,
> hundreds and hundreds of all sorts of people, going up to the
> temple of their Lord, with all their difficulties, trials and
> sorrows. I saw it full of people, dropping in at all hours of the
> day and night. It was never dark, it was lighted all night and all
> day, and often and often tired bits of humanity swept in. And
> I said to them as they passed: 'Where are you going?' And they
> said only one thing: 'This is our home. This is where we are
> going to learn of the love of Jesus Christ. This is the Altar of
> our Lord where all our peace lies.' It was all reverent and full of
> love and they never pushed me behind a pillar because I was
> poor. And day by day they told me the dear Lord's Supper was
> there on His Altar waiting to be given. They spoke to me two
> words only, one was the word 'Home' and the other was
> 'Love'.[9]

The variety of visitors to cathedrals today demonstrates that
cathedrals are living churches, rooted in living communities. In
Norwich we seek, through the building itself, to see how we
might better make clear the message of the Gospel through the
building.

Notes

1. James Mackey, *Jesus: The Man and the Myth*, London: SCM Press, 1979, p. 159
2. *The Diary of the Reverend Francis Kilvert, Selections*, Jonathan Cape, 1944, 1978,
   p. 97 (Wednesday 21 December 1870)
3. Peter Brown, *The Cult of the Saints*, London: SCM Press, 1981, p.86
4. *Ibid*, pp. 40–1
5. *One in Hope*, London: CTS/SPCK, 1989, p. 21

6. George Guiver CR, *Company of Voices*, London: SPCK, 1988, p. 96
7. Philip Toynbee, *Part of a Journey*, London: Collins, 1981, pp. 197–8
8. Philip Larkin, *Collected Poems*, London: Faber, 1988, pp. 97–8
9. Quoted in Alan Wilkinson, *Dissent or Conform*, London: SCM Press, 1986, p. 113